Simple
Isn't
Easy

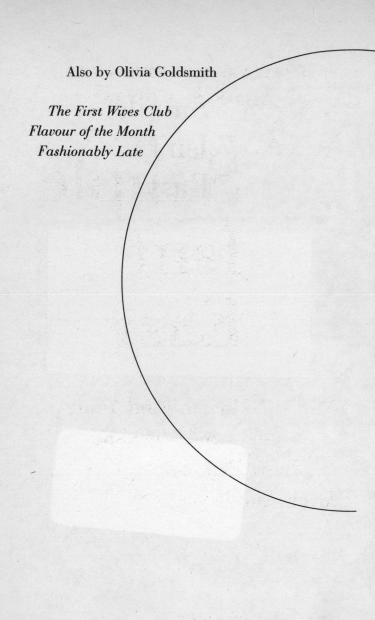

OLIVIA GOLDSMITH WITH
AMY FINE COLLINS

Simple Isn't Easy

How to Find Your Personal Style and Look Fantastic Every Day!

HarperCollins*Publishers*

To Barbara Turner, my stylish sister
And to Amy, who made this book simple
– but not easy.   O.G.

Erika Fine, my big sister
And to Olivia, who made this book easy
– but not simple.   A.F.C.

HarperCollins*Publishers*
77–85 Fulham Palace Road,
Hammersmith, London W6 8JB

A Paperback Original 1996
9 8 7 6 5 4 3 2 1

Copyright © Olivia Goldsmith & Amy Fine Collins 1996

Olivia Goldsmith and Amy Fine Collins assert the moral right to
be identified as the authors of this work

A catalogue record for this book
is available from the British Library

ISBN 0 00 638729 2

Set in Bauer Bodoni

Printed in Great Britain by
HarperCollinsManufacturing Glasgow

Contents

Some Notes Before We Begin

'Beauty of style and harmony and grace and good rhythm depend on simplicity.'

– PLATO

*T*his book began when I spent a year research-ing the fashion industry for my third novel, *Fashionably Late*. I spent a lot of time reading about or talking to designers, magazine editors, fashion writers, models, photographers, and others who create the clothes and the images that affect all of us. But far more interesting to me were the interviews with 'civilians' – normal women whom I met in the malls and shops across the US and the UK. Some women loved to shop. Others hated it. Some had unlimited budgets; others had to shop the sales and pinch pennies. But one thing I found consistently: no matter whom I spoke to, one irony stood out sharply. **There wasn't one woman who felt that she had the right clothes.** And I also found that shopping, the actual act of looking and purchasing, had become the Western woman's personal obsession.

(We are certainly worse in the US but Princess Diana and the culture of consumption is making definite inroads here.) I felt it was important to examine why so many women were obsessed with clothing and shopping. And I also had to examine the way the 'garmentos' – the uncreative, money-grubbing element of the fashion industry on both sides of the Atlantic – often feed that obsession or – worse – take advantage of it.

So I finished the novel, but I also began to examine the way I dressed, shopped and felt about clothes. The answers were complex and confusing, so I continued my research. Now, after an exhaustive eight-month process, I have reached a kind of personal fashion enlightenment. Like all enlightenment, it is simple – but not easy. It didn't happen overnight and it wasn't exactly what I expected, but if you feel that you could and should look better dressed than you do, this *Simple Isn't Easy* approach to style may be the answer.

The second irony I discovered in my research was the key to it all: that those most knowledgeable in the fashion world didn't buy into all the trends and fads of fashion. It is their version of the doctor's 'clinical detachment' – to dress in a 'uniform' that did not distract them. Most of them had developed a style of their own, and stuck with it. It seemed to free them

from insecurity and the kind of fashion slavery the rest
of us were victims of, while at the same time it defined
them more effectively than the lush fashion photographs
they helped to design and publish. I was lucky enough
to interview some of the most knowledgeable people in
the fashion world. And I began to see that there was a
need for a book that would help today's women find a
way out of the maze that fashion has become.

I promise that by following a few simple (but not
necessarily easy) steps you can:

- Look better dressed each and every day
- Spend less time on dressing and shopping
- Spend less money on clothes
- Have better organized clothes and roomier closets
- Make some money in the process
- Help less fortunate people

No, I'm not suggesting joining a Carmelite convent
(although the monastic look *was* big a couple of seasons
ago). Nor that you forget about style and wear jeans and
sweatshirts for the rest of your life. It's my own belief
that the female of our species, from earliest times, has
had an instinctive, sensuous delight in ornamentation.
(I'm sure there were certain cave women who wouldn't
be caught dead in a fig leaf – they felt they were more
the bamboo type.) And I look on that as a uniquely

female, healthy and creative form of self-expression. But it is an impulse that has undone us, as I'll show you.

I also believe that style must come not from without, but within. As D. T. Suzuki wrote about Zen – but it applies equally to style – 'Zen in its essence is the art of seeing into the nature of one's being, and it points the way from bondage to freedom.' Each of us can find our own freedom and take back the pleasure that is our birthright. Style enlightenment – like the more profound Zen kind – can only be obtained through meditation and self-contemplation, rather than from a TV commercial, magazine layout or some other ultimately disappointing external source.

But I am smart enough to know what I *don't* know. Not only do I know that I can't (and won't) tell other women how to dress, I also knew I wasn't expert enough in the higher issues of aesthetics and style to undertake a project like this by myself. So I asked Amy Fine Collins, universally admired style editor of *Harper's Bazaar* and contributing editor at *Vanity Fair*, to help me. Her art and fashion history background, her unrivalled sense of style and her practical working knowledge of the fashion industry has helped to make this book what it is. So, though I use my voice throughout, Amy has written as much of the book as I have and edited every word.

Our purpose is to simplify issues for you about who you are and how you want to look. I know that simple isn't easy. Still, it seems to me that women in the Nineties – with both greater self-awareness and a greater ecological concern than ever before – are ready to step off the trend treadmill and, instead, acquire real and lasting personal style. We are not giving directions in this book, but rather pointing out much which you already know. We are not telling you what to wear, but rather giving you the tools to help you decide. We hope we are directing you to a path you have been seeking for some time. If this book helps you to find it, I'm glad.

Olivia Goldsmith

$\mathcal{E}$ ver since I was able to buckle my own shoes, and probably even before then, I have loved clothing. My favorite toys were Barbie, the ultimate fashion plate, and paper dolls, whose outfits I often drew myself. I remember with perfect clarity all of my mother's wardrobe from my childhood. (She had gone to Paris to study fashion, but wound up an art historian instead.) And to this day I recall events by recollecting what I wore on a particular occasion. Always I adored the beauty, magic, and fantasy of fashion magazines, never imagining that I would one day work for one. My Southern childhood encouraged a fondness for feminine fripperies, but never at the expense of my other interests.

It makes me sad that something that has been a great source of pleasure to me can cause confusion, unhappiness and anxiety in other women. Women are often misled into supposing that they should resemble the images in fashion magazines. This is a misunderstanding of their purpose. They are meant for inspiration, fantasy, and admiration, not for imitation. Every historical era needs its ideals of beauty. The ancient Romans had their sculptures of Venus, the Renaissance its icons of the

Madonna. But as these cultures were not consumer
societies, they regarded these feminine images as sensual
or spiritual paragons – visions to contemplate, not
emulate. All civilized societies need to generate images of
beauty, and these should be pleasurable, not threatening,
to behold. One aim of this book is to help you to
distinguish between the public ideal of beauty and your
own personal standard, and to dress and groom yourself
accordingly. Adorning oneself to enhance one's
attractiveness is a very basic, powerful urge. I hope that
instead of denying, thwarting, or abusing this instinct you
can cultivate and master it.

If you feel overwhelmed by too many choices, too many
images, and confused by conflicting needs to be an
individual yet conform to a peer group, you are not alone.
Even the designers and fashion editors who make and
present the clothes you see in shops and magazines are
baffled about why, given all the merchandise out there
and all the direction given by magazines, women still
have such trouble establishing a good-looking wardrobe.

Fashion has become so diverse and changes occur so
quickly that it is not surprising that women have lost
their bearings. Short and long hemlines, square-toed and
pointy shoes, dramatic and understated makeup can all
chicly coexist in one single season. It was easier to be

stylish when only one look at a time reigned supreme. But in the Sixties fashion dictates, along with so many other social institutions, were deemed obsolete and were overthrown.

Happily, we are not headed back to a time of universal conformity. So as long as fashion remains a large and varied garden from which you may pluck what you please, you might as well have a guidebook to lead you to what is best and most becoming for you. *Simple Isn't Easy* will help steer you away from disorder, disillusionment and disaster and toward a simpler, clearer, more stylish path.

After all, we do want to look our best. Our appearance should be a source of pride and pleasure to ourselves, and those around us. Feeling good about the way you look frees you to go about the business of your life with more confidence and satisfaction.

There is an art to being stylish, but not all of us are artists. A natural gift for fashion is as rare as a special talent for painting. Interestingly, many fashion professionals, myself included, are would-be artists who have transferred their creative energies from one field to the other. Expertise in both fashion and art requires a feeling for proportion, scale, composition, and color – a combination of heightened visual awareness, fearlessness, and rigorous self-scrutiny. Yet few women expect to be accomplished painters (otherwise how-to-draw books would be topping the best-seller lists). Why, then, do so many of us strive to be accomplished dressers?

Well, one good reason is that every one of us wears clothes. And don't you agree that, since getting dressed is an act that we all must perform at least once a day, it is better to go about it with enjoyment and self-awareness than with blindness and timidity? Achieving a sense of style is not only a wonderful gift to yourself, it is a generous gesture to all those who see you. We don't want to be like the child who thinks no one notices her just because she has shut her eyes. What's on your body communicates to the world what's on your mind.

I hope *Simple Isn't Easy* helps you to think more clearly about who you are and how you look. Whether your taste is conservative or flamboyant, your wardrobe is your most public and direct form of self-expression. The great news is that neither beauty, youth, nor sex appeal is necessary to achieve style. In fact, they can be a hindrance. And of all these traits, style alone endures. This is something to celebrate.

CHAPTER ONE

The Fashion Trap

or Why Most Women Don't Look Good

> *'Fashion is made
> to go out of fashion'*
> — COCO CHANEL

*I*S GETTING DRESSED
each morning a problem?
Do you hate what you see in
your closet or, worse yet, in your
mirror? How come?

I don't know about you, but these questions made me
take several steps backwards! If you're in doubt about
your own sense of style (and you must be or you
wouldn't have bought this book) try this tongue-in-
chic quiz.

Learn if You're Fashion Impaired, Savvy, or Middle Ground

	YES	NO

? Do you tell people that fashion doesn't interest you but secretly envy your friend with the beautiful wardrobe?

? Have you ever left the house with mismatched shoes on your feet?

? Are you ignored by sales clerks when you go to shop?

? Did you seriously consider re-wearing the bridesmaid dress from your best friend's wedding?

YES | NO

? Have you already forgotten what you were wearing yesterday?

? Do you consider *Country Life* a fashion magazine?

? Do occasions that require you to dress up make you shudder?

? Do you live in jogging suits even though you haven't been near a gym in months?

? Can you remember the last time you received a compliment for how you looked? (Was it in this decade?)

How to score the quiz

All 'no's = Good for you! Return this book! You already
have all the fashion savvy you need

1 – 3 'no's = Middle ground; This book can help

4 – 9 'yes's = Bad news: you are one of the fashion
impaired. You really need this book!

Well, how fashion savvy are you? Where do you fall on
the spectrum between Fashion Impaired and Super-
Stylish? Or do you fall off the chart completely?

It's a painful realization, but most of us don't look well
dressed. And this doesn't mean that we aren't wearing
fashionable clothes, or that we aren't trying. Actually,
some women try too hard and their desperation shows.
(But at least you have to give them special credit for
trying.)

In search of answers, I began to carefully observe
women. I saw women wearing beautiful clothes that fit
poorly, women wearing colors that complemented their
shoes but not their skin tone. I saw women who seemed
to have given up: I saw women whose outfits proclaimed
'More gold!' or 'More fabrics! More ruffles! More

sequins!'. They looked like dinnerplates piled with ice cream, chips and chocolate syrup – all flavor and no nourishment – which is to say 'No Taste'.

What, then, causes the problem? How had all of this come to pass? As I continued my research, three reasons became clear:

> Too Much Stuff
> The Influence Of Evil 'Garmentos'
> The Lack Of Concentration

Too Much Stuff

*O*ne of the answers is that modern women actually take dressing too much for granted and that, my dear, is part of the problem. For the first time in history, clothes are readily available off the rack. They are reduced to an impulse buy. This leads to too much stuff. In the past, right up to the early part of this century, clothes were made by the wearer or by seamstresses to order. This meant that women thought long and hard before they cut into that bolt of merino wool. They wore a mistake for years. In the eighteenth century, the emerging middle-class woman might have had only three or four dresses, adding one as another wore out. Now, too often, we try to solve wardrobe problems by throwing money at them. And, like most problems, money is not the solution. More stuff actually makes more style problems, not fewer.

It's an epidemic. When I appeared on the Richard and Judy Show, Judy Finnegan told me that even she had trouble keeping her wardrobe under control. And she has a staff to help her.

The Influence of Evil 'Garmentos'

We have all had the experience of closets stuffed with clothes, coupled with the feeling we have nothing to wear. How does it happen? It is not only the availability of ready-to-wear garments, or our lack of self-control.

For years I had heard the misguided theory that designers – usually, according to this theory, male and gay – hated women and came up with ridiculous designs to make us all look bad. (I even planned a character like that for my novel.) But what I found, in reality, was that designers – male and female, whatever their sexual orientation – seemed to like women and their vision was most often of a beautiful, fluid bonding of a woman with her clothes. Their designs may not always work, and some are certainly guilty of designing only for the ideal woman's body, (or an adolescent boy's!) but there is no hatred or conspiracy.

If there is a conspiracy, it does not come from the creative people in fashion. The designers, stylists, photographers, editors, and reporters that I met were all – to a greater or lesser degree – sincerely entranced with fashion. And they are most often stylish people that one could learn from, and who are usually happy to teach. But there is both cynicism and condescension toward women on the part of the businessmen who run the financial side of the industry. These guys – I call them 'garmentos' – spend their business lives hyping whatever products they are selling this season, getting them produced as cheaply as possible and pushing them into the stores. They exploit labor and their customers. Evil garmentos are not the rule, but they do exist, living and thriving in both the manufacturing and the retail side of the business. And we are their victims.

Now, I suppose they are no worse than businessmen in the tobacco industry: they have us hooked and they mean to make it pay. But they do so by advertising in a way that makes us feel inferior and fearful, if we don't get in line. They sell fashion instead of style. And you better know the difference! As Yves St Laurent put it, 'Fashion changes but style is eternal.' If you get trapped into buying this season's latest do-dah even though it doesn't suit you and you feel awful in it, it is only partly your fault. The evil garmentos have struck another victim down. We're going to tell you how to stop letting that happen. And how to save a lot of money.

Lack of Concentration

*M*oney aside for the moment, how much thought and effort do you want to put into your personal style?

For some women, like my friend Greta, a single mother and investment banker in the City, the answer is 'not a lot'. She's a no-nonsense, practical type. But the Gretas of the world still have a slight nagging feeling that they could look better than they currently do. For Vivian, a North London film student, almost any level of effort seems worth the reward of feeling and looking attractive and comfortable. If you fall into either category or, as is most likely, somewhere in the middle, the *Simple Isn't Easy* method will work for you. But remember that fashion and style are only as important as you want them to be.

It's my impression that women care a lot. But that does not mean that we know what to do about it. Why? the reluctance we have to focus deeply on how we want to look – considering what is possible and what is not. Perhaps it is only a question of time, or the lack of it, which prevents some of us from really scrutinizing our looks and our style. Perhaps it is simply easier to be blinded to our faults and limitations then to cope with them. Maybe it's an inability to see, or diagnose. And perhaps it is impossible not to be swayed by the evil garmentos. For whatever the reason, despite money spent, most women don't actually successfully focus on how they want to look or, if they do, they fail to come up with a plan to achieve that look.

I admit it isn't easy. In the past, even the recent past, women didn't work and spent more time at home in comfortable, not-for-public wear, like the housedress (remember them?). They 'got dressed' to be seen publicly and that meant they had both the blueprint on how they were expected to look and the time to take great care: even a generation ago, most women – not just the Royals – were taught to wear hats and gloves in public places. But with the evolution of the working woman, we got used to being seen in public and stopped preparing. After all, we have so much else to do now. That is the heart of the problem. *Because getting dressed in an attractive, appropriate, and comfortable way is a difficult task.*

I talked all of these insights over with Amy. She added the missing piece. In addition to too much stuff, evil garmentos, and the lack of concentration, she was surprised that many women didn't follow the three unwritten principles of taste. Unwritten principles? What unwritten principles? Was this some secret code that I, too, had been unaware of?

Actually, they are the building blocks this book is based on. That, and the practical hints I needed to achieve them. They are **appropriateness**, **understatement**, and **ease**.

UNWRITTEN PRINCIPLE OF TASTE 1

Appropriateness

Some women I saw at one shopping mall wore tarty clothes that had no sexual subtlety, while others wore corporate armorplates that had no subtle sexuality. While the tarty look may work on the fashion runway or at a sophisticated nightclub and asexuality is *de rigeur* on business women at board meetings, there in the mall 'shocking' looked pathetic and 'stuffy' looked like taxidermy.

'Appropriate style seems to vary more by region in the US than in the UK,' explained Chrissy Bourne, a Surrey housewife who has travelled extensively in the US. 'New York women dress very differently than those in Florida. In the UK the variation isn't so wide.'

Julia Eccles, a manager at Harrods, adds, 'Appropriateness of dress is essential as it makes the wearer feel comfortable and confident in any situation. Within the work environment, clothes can empower and be authoritative or alter the way colleagues view you.'

Appropriateness means more than dressing for the place and the occasion. It also means projecting a positive and accurate awareness of who you are. Some women with lively, interesting, kind and loving demeanors were dressed so drably that they seemed to disappear into a marshmallow blob of beige polyester and stonewashed denim, while others wore outfits so coordinated, so busy or so bold that they, too, vanished – whatever was special about their faces, personalities or presences drowned out by their outfits' roar.

The late Grace Kelly, Princess of Appropriateness (and Monaco), knew that in the U.S. appropriateness means blending in, whereas in European society it means sticking out a bit. So for everyday wear, as a debutante and then as an ingenue actress, she favored cashmere twinsets, white gloves, pearls and clean-scrubbed skin and hair. But once she was a princess, for social events or official occasions she donned a diamond tiara, upswept hair, and discreetly glamorous gowns.

UNWRITTEN PRINCIPLE OF TASTE 2

Understatement

The concept here is that you've got a statement to make and it's so worthwhile, it can speak gently; you don't need to knock everybody's eyes out to get it across. Understatement generally means choosing clean lines over choppy, fussy, elaborate silhouettes, using a few harmonious colors to good effect, and showing small splashes of brightness, dazzle, bare skin, etc. rather than oceans of anything. In other words, try to avoid looking like Edina from Absolutely Fabulous. Note that understatement does NOT mean self-effacement: 'I want to vanish so that no one notices how flawed I am' translates into 'Nobody has flaws but me', which is both unattractively self-pitying and grossly unobservant. Think of Cindy Crawford's mole. She kept it. She uses it to proclaim that she's unique. But you'll notice that she doesn't make a big deal of it by painting zillions of beauty marks all over. Designer Carolina Herrera has made polka dots her trademark – she even uses them on her perfume packages – but she uses them sparingly. You would never see this classic, serene beauty clownishy dressed in an overwhelming head-to-toe polka-dot statement.

UNWRITTEN PRINCIPLE OF TASTE 3

Ease and Grace

How do we define it? the appearance of being comfortable and confident, not only in your understated, appropriate outfit, but in Capital-L 'Life'. Early in her husband's presidency, Nancy Reagan wore her fastidious assemblages of matching buttons, jewels and shoes with as much aplomb as anyone could, but the obsessive coordination of it all was exhausting to behold, what we call 'too matchey-matchey'. If by chance she showed up at your flat you would expect her to start flicking soot flecks off the window sills. You could always tell that being judged by the public was torture for her.

Baroness Thatcher, on the other hand, used the conservative Aquascutum business suit to great effect. By combining both the masculine and feminine in her look and by appearing totally comfortable with it, she stressed her power.

Isabella Rossellini, the actress and model, always looks relaxed, whether she's in a bathing suit or an evening gown. It's not just because she's beautiful either; it's because she wears clothes that announce (quietly) that she feels good about how she looks. As one designer put it, 'an appearance of naturalness is essential to style'.

Why is it that so few of us have absorbed these principles, even if we have learned so many other of life's lessons? Part of the reason, I think, is that each of us is expected to reinvent the wheel. If you want to learn music, there are methods; you start with scales, master an instrument, and gradually increase your knowledge and ability until you can work your own variations on what has come before. But if you want to learn to dress with style, you're expected to invent yourself from whole cloth all on your own. Overwhelmed with choices and conflicting advice in newspapers, magazines and on TV, most women end up improvising variations on fashion's themes before they learn fashion's basics. Anyone can develop style, but if you're not, like Amy, born with it, and your job isn't in the performing or fine arts, the place to start is by evolving your personal version of good taste before attempting revisions of it. This doesn't mean dressing just like Grace, Cindy, Carolina or Isabella but it usually means mastering the principles that they embody: Quality, balance, awareness of self and place, subtlety, ease.

The Uniform

*H*ow to put this all into practice? The most fascinating thing I observed was that all of the stylish people in the fashion business had stopped following fashion! What they had instead was what I call 'a uniform'. Though it varied widely from person to person, each of them had selected what worked best for them and then seemed to stick with it. This gave them not only ease in dressing, but also a visible identity. This book aims to help you do the same. It means you must give up promiscuous shopping, following fads, and self-hatred. It means you must take a clear and accurate look at yourself and the way you live. It means you must clean out your closet and admit your mistakes.

But what you'll get in return is a clear sense of your own uniform and a simplicity in both getting dressed and in your looks. With luck this will develop even further into your own personal style.

We have chosen not to make *Simple Isn't Easy* a book of 'Do's and 'Don't's because we both hate the idea of commandments (Amy's first instinct is to bend, twist, break and challenge rules) – and because we want to encourage you to find your own personal style. Yet, as

you may have noticed, at the same time we don't
endorse an 'anything goes' outlook on getting dressed.
We do have opinions, and strong ones, on what
constitutes personal style. We are, for example, against
any individual looks that are self-destructive, self-
denying, or that arise out of fear or ignorance. The
'I-don't-know-anything-about-style-but-I-know-what-
I-like' attitude does not work for us either. If you make
judgments and choices about clothing, you should know
why you make them. If you know not just what you like
but why you like it, then you have learned something
not only about fashion but also about style – and
yourself. Finally, remember here that we are talking
about clothes, but not only about clothes. In the words
of Valentino, 'Quality in fashion is determined by
workmanship, beautiful fabrics, the finishing and
details. But often, all this does not add quality to a
woman herself. For a woman quality is something
within her.'

CHAPTER TWO

Fear and Clothing

or Pitiful Pitfalls

*'Were the diver to think on
the jaws of the shark he
would never lay hands
on the precious pearl'*

– SA'DI

*N*OW THAT WE'VE
separated the good guys from
the bad guys and handed you
some guiding principles, we'd also
like to acquaint you with some common
pitfalls that may undermine your best efforts at
style. We've identified a number of bad, unacceptable
reasons that women may have for dressing as they do – and
the kinds of looks that arise from them. In this chapter
we're going to define them. If you recognize your mode in
one of these categories, it will be the first step toward
finding your way out, and into a stylishness all your own.

Now, we're not going to give you news about what height heels are in or out. Instead, what each of these categories has in common – and why you should steer clear of them – is that they all arise from FEAR, a crippling and blinding emotion.

Personal style invariably begins from security. Do you, instead of dressing in what pleases you, succumb to these fears? Are you:

Afraid of Looking Too Rich?

*S*ometimes called 'reverse chic' or 'reverse snobbery', this look is popular among old money or guilty liberals and/or feminists. You know the look: ugly polyester dresses instead of lovely silk; out-of-date, frayed frumpiness that does not make the wearer look better (or fool anyone about her solvency). 'Dressing down', is really just a way of putting yourself down.

Afraid of Looking Too Poor?

*T*his fear usually results in piling on glittering junk – gilt buttons, knock-offs of more expensive garments, scarves, and shoes. The result is almost always the reverse of the intended effect. Trying desperately to imitate an expensive style you can't afford only makes your attempt look cheap compared to the real thing. Try, instead, for something genuine and within your means.

Afraid of Looking Too Conformist?

*Y*ou've seen this: it results in a detestable fake rebel effect: body piercing, tattoos, too much leather, unwashed jeans, all imitating an authentic rebel style from the past (hippie, beatnik, punk). Ironically, 'rebel without a cause' looks are often the most conformist looks around. (Adolescents often put themselves in this trap, but they're excused. They can plead raging hormones and the painful slide into adulthood.) If you simply like tattoos, terrific. But if you think you're being avant garde, ask yourself this: how can you be a nonconformist when thousands of others are also sporting holey blue jeans, nose rings, shaved heads, and the exact same look?

Afraid of Looking Too Out of the Ordinary?

*A*h, the deadly corporate clone or suburban Stepford Wife effect! Norma Major has very much succeeded in updating her image from this, though she still looks a bit 'housewife-made-good'. We know that many professions, offices, and even neighborhoods have an unwritten dress code and we're all for appropriateness but we challenge you to be as creative and individual as possible within that code. If you look at a group of uniformed school girls you will notice dozens of incredibly imaginative but subtly individual touches that make some uniforms more personal – variations in skirt length, sock folding, collar shape, or just the manner of rolling up sleeves. Apply this same principle to your own peer group's appropriate gear.

Afraid of Looking Too Sexy?

I'm a victim of this fear, which all too often results in loose, shapeless, buttoned-up, uptight or mannish clothes. In the corporate world I hoped it would fend off harassment. (It didn't.) In my private life, I thought it would camouflage my weight and make me more appealing. Boy, was that wrong! With this kind of fear, a woman looks stiff or unsensual, unapproachable and undesirable – not just to men, but to other women, children, and pets. (Well, actually, my beagle still loved me.)

The bad news, girls, is that women in the UK are famous for this fear. If American women are laughed at for being styleless, you're sneered at by the French for being sexless in your dress.

Carole Ann Rice, a Birmingham journalist, and good friend, pointed this pitfall out to me. Carole wears form-fitting sweaters and cinched-waisted slacks. She never looks cheap or obvious. 'I feel comfortable looking hot. We should be free to express ourselves this way. It's fun.' And it definitely is Carole Ann.

Afraid of Not Looking Sexy Enough?

*Y*ou know what this results in, something like Patsy on AbFab. Don't you feel sorry for the would-be vamps out there, who usually model themselves after some soap or rock star or other such unrealistic role model? Too much hair, noisy jewelry, cheap perfume, ill-fitting, tight clothes. If that describes you, get a grip! Men will know you're a woman without the rubber skirt and the tube top. Pierre Cardin, the great French designer, knew all about this fear. 'It's stupid if you need to see everything that a woman is,' he said. 'You must use your imagination. If you see immediately, the charm is finished, you know. It's like a book. If you know everything immediately, it is not exciting.' Sexiness is about mystery, not about being obvious.

Afraid of Standing Out?

*A*lso known as the 'Who, me?' or wallflower effect, this fear usually results in slovenliness, bad posture, and faded, dreary colors that blend into skin-tones. If, when you sit on a beige sofa in a waiting room, you become invisible, you're a victim of this fear. Elegance can be quiet, but it must also be confident.

Afraid of Blending In?

*T*he opposite of the above mentioned 'Who, me?' syndrome, this fear results in attention-getting but unflattering hats, general loudness in color of clothes and makeup, clanging jewelry, lots of rhinestones, noisy high heels, flashing knick-knacks on shoes, belts, and even sweatshirts. For victims of this problem, remember this: Sometimes the best way to be heard is to whisper.

Afraid of Looking Too Old?

*W*ell, in this youth-obsessed society, aren't we all? But when that fear results in dressing like a teenager when you're middle-aged, you've got a problem. (Sometimes even teenagers should not dress like teenagers!) Dressing much younger than your years only makes you look older by contrast – just like lying about your age does. This fear can also have you jumping on trends without really pausing to consider whether they are flattering or appropriate. Who wants to look like mutton dressed as lamb? And who do you fool? Youthfulness is a question of attitude and energy, not young clothing.

Afraid of Looking Too Young?

*M*ost of us outgrow this by our late twenties but, whenever it occurs, it results in a forced sophistication that looks awkward and disguises the true appeal of youth. Common mistakes from this fear include too much 'good' jewelry, fur coats, very high

heels, too much makeup – a kind of jailbait effect.
Learn from your elders, but don't dress like them – yet.
There's plenty of time for that. As the French say,
'Elegance is the privilege of age.'

Afraid of Looking Too Casual?

*H*ey, Little Miss Perfect, loosen up! (Even if your 'loosening up' is as carefully calculated as your every outfit.) Unbutton a button, push up your sweater sleeves, slacken the knot tying your scarf. Good clothes are designed to move, to be fluid. Otherwise you look like a prim, flawlessly wrapped gift package with nothing inside.

Afraid of Looking Too Formal?

*G*od, those women in bicycle shorts and trainers at the museum, in anorak at the theater! Show a little respect for the hostess of your party, the city you're visiting, for the old friends you're meeting for dinner – and for yourself. The sloppy, dirty, messy, 'I just got back from an Outward Bound week and haven't had time to change' look just doesn't work, except in the wilderness.

Afraid of Seeming Too Stylish?

*Y*es, there can be a fearful overreaction to the latest issue of *Elle*. (This is not a new problem. One of Edith Wharton's characters in *The Age of Innocence* was so afraid of appearing too fashionable she used to store her Paris purchases in a box for a year before she wore them!) If you become terrified and overwhelmed by the new, it may mean you'll never change your style – even when you've outgrown it. You'll be lost in a time warp with your too-short coat and too-long dress. This fear produces women who seem to derive no pleasure from clothing, or for that matter from life. Consider the words of Joubert: 'There may be less vanity in following the new modes than in adhering to the old ones.'

Afraid of Seeming Too Unstylish?

*T*he reverse of the above, it results in slavish fashion faddism as a substitute for style – piling on everything you saw in an advertisement or a catwalk shot. It makes you look like you have no judgment of your own. And it costs piles of money to keep on the fashion treadmill.

Afraid You're Trying Too Hard?

*I*f you look like you don't care, then you seem as if you don't care about yourself either. So why should anyone care about you? Take pride in your appearance. There's no shame in it, no matter what you've been told. Put on some makeup, press your clothes, try on a pair of comfortable heels.

Afraid You're Not Trying Hard Enough?

*I*f you try too hard then your anxiety and tension show. Too much concern about matching colors, patterns and textures looks fussy, overwrought, and frightened. Relax, loosen up, eliminate, be sparing. Dress for who you are, not for whom you want others to mistake you. Giorgio Armani, my Zeus in the Pantheon of designer Gods, told me, 'Do not force yourself to look like something you're not. Naturalness is synonymous with style.'

Finally, who is the audience you are trying to please?
The only valid answer, as far as we're concerned, is
YOURSELF. You must recognize your own fears and
overcome them. If you are a victim of any of the fears
we have described, we can help you eliminate them but
only you can do it for yourself. As Julia Eccles of
Harrods puts it: 'To dress stylishly, forget fashion,
develop your own look that suits . . . and be yourself,
don't follow anyone else.' What we are proposing is a
way to feel and look better with less effort, but it
requires self-examination and mindfulness. In the rest
of *Simple Isn't Easy* we suggest a combination of
meditations and actions to achieve a more stylish and
simplified wardrobe.

CHAPTER THREE

Simple Isn't Easy

or The Zen Approach to Style

'It's better to lose than acquire'
– BORIS PASTERNAK

W ELL, AMY
helped me to discover the
principles of style, and even how
they might be broken. And she led me
away from some fear-induced pitfalls. Though
she left me with some clear, gorgeous visions in my
head, I still had a murky mess in my closet. Because,
my friend, I had shopped. And, like most of us, I
had shopped badly and too often.

I didn't live at Harvey Nichols the way Patsy and Edina seem to do, but I never made a trip to London without a heavy day spent on Oxford Street. They knew my name at Selfridges – and I didn't have to pay VAT!

With Amy's enlightenment guiding me like a golden beacon, I came to some important truths about what I feel best dressed in. I decided, once and for all, that I had more than enough. That I would do my shopping in my closet, and find myself. And that meant a task almost more daunting than cleaning out the Augean stables. I lead the way, but you can do it too. Here, in seven simple (but not easy) steps you too can achieve simplicity and style.

1   Try On Everything You Own

  2   Decide on a Look

    3   Contemplate the Tragedies

  4   Further Sort the Garments from Your 'Keep' Pile

1   Survey What You Have Wrought

  6   Learn the Zen Philosophy of Fashion

7   Practice Wearing This Stuff for a Month

STEP ONE

Try On Everything You Own

The first step is, as always, the most important. And the hardest. Most women – those of us who are not gifted with natural chic like Amy – spend a lifetime trying to evolve a look and never really succeed. But now you will. It may not, in the end, be your only look, or perhaps even your ultimate look. But you will pick one and stick with it for a while.

The way I decided was by trying on just about everything I had. God, how exhausting. But do it. This is the key to everything. What an exercise! (If you need any more motivation to simplify, this should do the trick.) I put a whole morning aside and I wasn't done by lunch (and I get up very early!) So, as you move through the nightmare of your closet, **make two piles – the good and the bad**. Looks I liked, I put in one pile; those I didn't, I put in another. (Don't worry about the reject pile for now. We'll get back to it.) When I was done, I had lunch and a drink. I needed it. When I had strength for it, I

went back and once again tried on everything
that I had put in the 'Good Look Pile'. This is
where the buck stops – the end of the road. Only
keep in that pile what you can and will wear
happily and stylishly.

Now, I know this is the part where all you
squirrels out there get nuts. 'What?' you cry.
'Get rid of this fabulous designer silk body suit
that I bought in 1977 at seventy-five per cent
off?' I admit, I was hyperventilating when I got
to this point in the process. But did I say that
you had to get rid of anything permanently? No!
For now, make a pile of stuff that doesn't work.
I promise, you don't have to get rid of it! Just
take some cardboard cartons (lots of them,
probably) and start to put stuff there **for the
time being**.

STEP TWO

Decide on a Look

So, now you've done a preliminary sort. Great. But difficult as it was, that isn't the hard part. Now you have to decide what you learned from your experience. I discovered that I always feel best in neutrals and I don't like fuss. No ruffles, no fringe, no sequins. It just ain't me.

Believe me, it wasn't easy, and I certainly don't know what looks good on you (though Amy probably does). If you don't have a clue about what looks good on you, and what feels comfortable and what works in your life, you might need professional help. (More about that later.) I contend, however, that most of us do know, but we forget, or don't think about it, or get seduced when we shop. For most of us, it isn't a question of money or taste. It's really more a lack of focus. So take a long cool look at yourself. Remember the advice of fashion expert Diana Vreeland: 'You've got to think of yourself and not how everyone else is dressed.'

Robert Burns called it a gift only the gods could give us: to see yourself as others see you. Well, I have a sneaking suspicion that dour old Mr Burns did not have fashion in mind when he penned those famous lines. But good poetry, like good wardrobe advice, always has a universal application, right?

So hold on to the Good Look Pile to assess again in the next chapter. Meanwhile . . .

STEP THREE

Contemplate the Tragedies

That scary bad pile has got to be addressed.
Maybe, you think, there are treasures lurking
there. Maybe you should keep it all. Well, not
until you go through this process.

• GET RID OF THE REAL MISTAKES

I'm embarrassed to admit that there were a few
things with the price tags still on them. Good
money paid, stuff never worn. If even Amy's
done it, we've all done it. So be brave. Admit
your worst mistakes. And try to see a pattern in
your past errors. Courage. Remember the words
of Georges Santayana: 'Those who do not study
history are condemned to repeat it.'

• OUT WITH THE THINGS THAT DON'T FIT

'It's nice but it always was too tight under the
arms.' Out! 'I can't button the waist but I can
wear a long blouse.' Out! 'It's pretty but I always
have to pin the neckline or a breast falls out.'
Goodbye! And last, that terribly poignant,

painful category: 'Once I could fit into a size ten. Maybe I will again.' Ah! If only we could all be like Amy who's been the same size since she was fifteen. Well, forget about it. Get rid of it. When you hit size ten again, (dream on!) you have our permission to go on a shopping spree.

• OUT WITH THE COSTUMES

As Marcel Proust wrote, 'Very few women are suited to old-fashioned dresses with an air of the theater or costume ball.' Unless you've decided the costume look is absolutely you, get rid of the MGM casting wardrobe. I had to let go of two Victorian-looking white Laura Ashleys (I'm not sixteen any more – or one hundred and ten pounds!), a señorita crinoline (nice concept, but I bear no resemblance to the late Carmen Miranda), as well as an antique Japanese kimono jacket and an Indian fringed shawl. (At this point Amy became inspired too and made a museum donation of some vintage couture that had made her look like a Fifties fashion photo.) How does all this junk accumulate? The fact is, piece by piece, each of these has a certain charm. But can they be integrated into a workable, simple wardrobe? No, unless you're Danny LaRue.

I did once have a co-worker, Mimi, who was a real character – a different character every day. One day she was an English schoolgirl, the next a biker babe, the next a Southern belle with petticoats. It was interesting, but it was a full-time job and, not surprisingly, no one at our office ever took her seriously. And she had to turn her entire apartment into a closet for her props and accessories. (She kept her shoes in the oven.) Needless to say, Mimi had no time for a real career. (She was working as a temp.) Unless you want to be Mimi, **put the costumes in a box.**

● GET RID OF THE SENTIMENTAL FAVORITES

Yeah, yeah, you wore it the night he proposed. But the marriage failed, it never looked good on you, it doesn't fit any more, and it's still there, even though he isn't! Get rid of the bridesmaid's dress, the holiday souvenir T-shirt, the college sweatshirt. Is this a closet or a diary? I asked myself. Have a separate box for these keepsakes, if you must. Think of them as memorabilia, not clothes. You may decide to keep them forever, but for now, out of your closet and into the box.

• UNLOAD THOSE REALLY EXPENSIVE THINGS THAT JUST DON'T WORK

I don't care if it's Versace and the most expensive skirt you ever bought – you look like a hippo in it, so put it aside. Somehow, the price ticket often makes us think we should wear something, even if it looks lousy. My favorite trousers in the universe were twenty-six pounds at The Gap. They're perfect, stylish and comfortable, and the designer version at four times the price never fit. (Amy got rid of some expensive Italian designer T-shirts with a badly cut V-neck and started wearing Hanes boys' T-shirts from Woolworth's instead.)

Okay. When I was done with this process I admit I was feeling lightheaded. I had filled six boxes. Take your boxes and put them out of sight. If you're feeling shaky and insecure – like someone in drug withdrawal – repeat to yourself, 'I still have all my clothes, only they're not all in my closet.'

STEP FOUR

Further Sort the Garments from Your 'Keep' Pile

The aim here is to put the good stuff together into outfits. I decided on a general outfit as my best look: a blouse, jacket and narrow-legged trousers. How did I decide? Here's a clue: I already had six of each. What do you keep buying and wearing? However, you, like me, will probably find that all tapered trousers were not created equal. This step is all about selectivity. And, to be honest, there were other things I liked. So, I went through the pile again and began yet another cleaning-out process. The point is to find your personal uniform.

If you find this difficult (my girlfriend, Margret, called from Suffolk crying over this one) here are some basic guidelines:

• PUT ASIDE STUFF THAT YOU STILL LIKE BUT THAT DOESN'T WORK WITH ANYTHING ELSE

Who knows? You may decide later that the sophisticated knit suit *isn't* your basic unit, but for now, we're pretty convinced that those cowboy boots won't work with it. So put them in another box.

• OUT WITH THE THINGS THAT NEED FIXING

There was this whole category of stuff that I didn't wear because:

▶ I lost an irreplaceable button

▶ a zipper was broken

▶ a back hem was coming down

▶ jacket pockets were torn

▶ a seam was opened, or needed to be taken up/let down/taken in/let out.

Some, I'm embarrassed to say, had been hanging like that for a long time (like half a decade for the Chanel-like sweater minus a Chanel-like button). But some, unfixed as they were, I loved and I decided they were part of my basic look. So I fixed them (see chapter thirteen). I mean, when you've got twenty pairs of assorted trousers, there's no hurry to fix the broken zipper in one. When you pare down to six, there is. And then I didn't have that awful experience of getting dressed – only to find my trousers were torn and I had to start over.

Now arrange the clothes into the best possible single combination. Which blouse with which pair of cropped trousers? **Make outfits**. And if you find you have a bottom without a top or a dress that needs a jacket – hang it on the side. You'll have to get something that works with it or eliminate it. Arrange the rest of the closet.

Speaking of closets, step back and take a look at the little darling.

STEP FIVE

Survey What You Have Wrought

Oh, my God! You're left with nothing to wear!
If you're like me, by now you will probably be
panic-stricken when you look into your newly
lean closet. At this point it is helpful to
remember the immortal words of Coco Chanel,
'Simplicity doesn't mean poverty.' Amy says that
opening a closet door should be like arriving at a
really good party where everyone you see is
someone you like. At this point it should be at
least half as crowded as it was. But now it's
organized by outfits. Complete units. Easy to
see, easy to wear. I can get dressed in seven
minutes. And like what I have on. In fact, I dress
in half the time I used to and look twice as good.
But:

- DON'T GIVE/THROW AWAY ANYTHING YET

Who knows? You may have made a mistake.
Nothing gets thrown away. Wait. After Chapters
Four, Five and Six, you may want or need to go
through the process again.

And if you still have nagging doubts about some
of your remaining clothes, why not have a friend
try some of them on so you can see how they look
from a more objective perspective? Amy
discovered through this method that some of her
clothes that were almost right for her were
actually perfect for her friend Miriam, who wears
the same size and has a similar (but not identical)
style. 'It's happened more than once,' Amy says.
'The near misses in my closet are hits with my
best friend. Now Miriam, her sister Vivian and I
circulate clothes out of our closets to one another.'

• ORGANIZE WHAT YOU'VE GOT

You know how to do this: trousers in one section,
blouses in another, skirts in a third, etc. Right?
Wrong! Only closet salesman will push this on
you. I've discovered that 'coordinates' often
don't coordinate and 'separates' usually stay
separate. All beige blouses don't go with all grey
skirts. So, try to arrange complete units: blouse
with trousers with belt with scarf with jacket. All
together. Ready to grab and put on at a
moment's notice. Yes, you do lose some flexibility
but, if you've done your homework what you
gain is your ultimate, most polished looks.

What did I wind up with? Don't – please don't –
use this as a guide for yourself. Remember, I'm a
childless, forty-year-old writer who spends
eighty per cent of her life at home and twenty
per cent with my publishers or on book tours.
My list is only that. Mine. This isn't about
copying, it's about evolving. With that said,
here's what can be found in my lean closet:

Seven Pairs Of Black Trousers - The basic item
I decided to use as my foundation. Two silk, two
wool, a tuxedo stripe, one Issey Miyake (bought
years ago in a sale), and cotton/Lycra Gap pants
that fit like a dream.

Two Black Skirts - One straight, one pleated.
For less casual wear.

Six White (or Off-white) Silk Blouses - OK, I
admit it: I'm a silk-shirtaholic. So lock me up!
But it is *my* uniform, and you can only wear 'em
once before washing or cleaning them.

Three Patterned Blouses - Each one goes with almost all the slacks, but I did pair them up into outfits as alternatives to the plain blouses.

Four Blazers - All of them dark neutral colours: olive, khaki, aubergine and sage green. I like them with black trousers.

Three Handknit Sweaters - I wear them when a blazer is too formal.

This gives you an idea of how much I had before I started simplifying! I think I can do with less, but so far this is really working for me.

STEP SIX

Learn the Zen Philosophy of Fashion

This is the really important part. Remember the words of fashion doyen Diana Vreeland: 'Elegance is refusal'. If you don't get this you're doomed to repeat the cycle over and over again, moving through malls in a fog, restocking your closets, a slave to the evil garmentos, lost forever in fashion purgatory, reincarnated again and again. When I shop do I still look at the marked-down, lime green raw silk jacket with the polka dot rosette? Or the orange suede swing coat? I admit I linger over them longingly – and then I leave 'em! I have changed the way I dress and the way I shop. Designer Bob Mackie put it well: 'Too many women follow the fashion. You'd do better to stick with a style and only add a piece or two a year.' So, look in the mirror and repeat your first fashion mantra:

MANTRA 1: I want to look stylish. To do it,
I must keep things simple.

Princess Diana can have an outfit for every
occasion but she has an (almost) unlimited
budget and a staff of three who clean and press
and sort and hang her clothes. And it's her job
to change her clothes twelve times a day!

So now take a deep breath and repeat your
second, third and fourth mantra:

MANTRA 2: A full closet does not mean stylish.

MANTRA 3: Shopping all the time does not
mean stylish.

MANTRA 4: Changing my look every season (or
month, or week, or day!) does not mean stylish.

Repeat these mantras twenty-five thousand times.
Repeat them as you read a fashion magazine at
the dentist's. Repeat them as you walk past
department store windows. Repeat them as you
go through the rest of this sorting out process.

STEP SEVEN

Practice Wearing This Stuff for a Month!

With my new, pared down, only-the-best closet, I immediately found it easier and more fun to dress. In the past, each morning I'd begin by selecting a skirt or dress or pair of slacks. Then I'd get confused as I scanned the whole closet for the blouse or jacket or sweater to go with it. Now I simply pick a whole outfit. And that gives me the luxury of time to think about the telling details. A black jeweled belt and matching socks. Or a chunky chain and a glint of Lycra stocking underneath. I'm looking good. Honestly!

Progress Report

It is now seven months into my *Simple Isn't Easy* approach to style. I know that I spend less time dressing and I also believe I look a lot more stylish. It's a discipline I can keep to, with a few slips and corrections. My sister even said to me, 'You look so nice lately. Have you lost weight?'

BINGO!

CHAPTER FOUR

Self-Assessment

or Mirror, Mirror on the Wall

'Know yourself, then create yourself'
– MARY McFADDEN

'It is as hard to see one's self as to look backwards without turning around'
– HENRY DAVID THOREAU

WELL, YOU'VE cleaned out your closet and you feel better for it, but how are you sure you've selected the real 'you'? I was lucky. I had Amy's help. But how do you do it? As Teilhard de Chardin said, 'The whole of life lies in the verb *seeing*.'

Really looking at yourself is a difficult skill to learn. Most of us tend to be either too self-critical or ignore the 'problem areas' we ought to deal with. Both are deadly. So let us share the secret of style self-discovery. It's called a mirror.

Goethe wrote that 'thinking is more interesting than knowing, but less interesting than looking'. This chapter is all about looking and learning to see. Can you imagine that mirrors did not begin to become widely available until the seventeenth century? Do you now wish that you could time travel back to a no-mirror world? Then you really need to pay attention to this chapter. Because today there is no escaping your reflection. Even the beautiful Narcissus of Greek mythology managed to find a lake to look into so he could fall in love with himself. (Unfortunately a lot of these Narcissus guys are still alive and walking amongst us. In fact, I think I saw one the last time I was at my local restaurant on the Fulham Palace Road, ignoring his date and preening in the looking glass.) We are not encouraging empty vanity here, but realistic self-awareness. Remember, even if there were a law against lakes and mirrors, your reflection would still be everywhere. It is in the effect you make on other people, from perfect strangers to imperfect husbands.

We should be grateful for the modern world's technological self-reflecting wonders: mirrors, cameras and video recorders. Because through these devices we can learn to assess ourselves clinically and objectively, so that we may never fear a camera or mirror – or the gaze of another's eyes – again.

Mirrors

*C*onsider your mirror not as an enemy but as your strongest ally. No fooling. It has traits that even your best friend might lack. It never tells you you're looking good when you're not, nor will it enviously tell you you look bad (or that euphemism 'tired') when you don't. Why is it that Amy's baby girl, Flora, knows instinctively that the mirror is her friend while grown-up women don't? When Flora sees her reflection she grins and laughs at her image and strokes the glass with pleasure – sometimes she even kisses it! Weren't we all like that once? What happened? Our guess is that somewhere along the way we've developed some ideal that we aspire to – suggested by movies, ads, boyfriends, parents etc. – and that most often this just doesn't correspond with what we see looking back at us.

By following our self-assessment plan, you'll either: lose that old counterproductive ideal and replace it with another, fulfill your ideal (or a realistic facsimile), or accept yourself exactly as you are and become comfortable and happy with that image. It is necessary, though difficult, to do one of these things because otherwise you (and I) are doomed to eternal dissatisfaction. And it all begins with self-assessment.

The most important step for self-assessment is to **set up some full-length mirrors permanently in your house that give you a front, side, and back view of yourself.** Of all the suggestions we have to offer in this book, this one might rank as number one. We are not paper dolls with only one frontal view, (even if you want to be!). Close your eyes and for a second picture your mother, your child, or someone else you see often. I guarantee that you did not think of them face-on with their arms dropped stiffly to their sides, but in movement, from an angle. Well, for better or worse, that is how the rest of the world pictures and sees you. Clothes should be a moving, fluid, three dimensional part of that picture. As Yves St Laurent put it, 'I like to watch the way a model moves in my clothes, the way she gives them life, or if they are wrong, still born, the way her life rejects them.'

When they see a woman dressed inappropriately for their age, their figure, or the occasion, all the fashion designers Amy knows make the same remark: 'Did she look in the mirror before she went out?' Similarly, Graydon Carter, the dapper editor-in-chief of *Vanity Fair* magazine quips, 'If people really studied themselves in a three-way mirror you'd see a lot less Lycra on the street.'

Now, that isn't to scare you, or make you feel you must dress to please either fashion pros or magazine editors. We're only asking you to see yourself clearly and then make the decision about how you want to be seen. You don't have to please everyone, but you ought to be aware of how you look, and how you look to others. Then decide how you want to present yourself.
So, be courageous! Stand before your three-way mirror, in a leotard, your bra and underpants, or – if you can bear it – in the nude. Consider this old French saying: 'Women dress well in countries where they undress often.'

Now ask yourself these questions:

~ *Do You Love Everything You See?*

If the answer is a resounding 'yes', you may have
bought the wrong book. You can wear anything. If
your answer is 'no', proceed with the following:

~ *What Do You Like Best About What You See?*

It could be your long neck, your shapely calves, your
full cleavage or your height. These are your strong
points, the ones you'll want your clothes to
emphasize. And you **do** have some. Focus on the
positive.

~ *What Do You Like Least?*

Your short neck, your shapeless calves, your boney
cleavage, your height. These aren't tragedies; they are
merely target areas that you want clothes to
camouflage or minimize.

Don't stop yet! The operation is painful but you'd have
a quadruple bypass to save your heart, wouldn't you?
This is only slightly more painful, and hey! at least
nobody is watching you.

See your total being, now, not just the parts. Yes, women
are objectified by society and by themselves as well, but
remember how many different parts of that 'object' –
yourself – there are. If an artist were to paint a full-
length portrait of you, do you think she would just look
at your bust, your waist, your hips, your face, and your
hair? Of course not – she would scrutinize all that lay in
between – your ankle bones, your fingers, the curve of
your shoulder, the shape of your earlobes. So why
reduce yourself to the sum of a few parts? Almost every
woman we know – whatever her shape or weight or age
– hates her thighs, and thinks her bust is either too large
or too small. Forget those most obvious categories and
see the whole. Your 'measurements' are not a tripartite
sum – even a tailor knows that.

No one is consistently perfect, or consistently imperfect
everywhere. I was so saddened to read in Gloria
Steinem's memoir that the only part she liked about

herself was her hands. They are indeed lovely, but so is so much else. So focus not just on the obvious – those parts that we typically obsess over – like thighs and breasts and buttocks. Think of the whole picture.

Also bear in mind that adopting good posture can make your whole physical presence more attractive. As Lucinda Chambers, *Vogue*'s senior fashion stylist, says: 'Never forget posture, I've never seen a stylish woman who slouches.' You'd be surprised how many 'flaws' improve when you stand the way a dancer does, with chest high, head straight on, and back straight. It will at least give you the illusion of confidence and poise – not to mention that clothes will also hang better on you!

To help you discover your whole self as well as neglected parts of your anatomy, which may in fact be points of beauty, and to help you see yourself in a new, more enlightened way, we've devised a self-assessment chart. Rate yourself, as you stand before your mirror, for the body parts we listed.

AMY AND OLIVIA'S POSITIVE ASSESSMENT LIST

	Love It	*Don't Like It*	*Neutral*
Ears			
Jawline			
Neck			
Shoulders			
Back – Upper			
Upper Arms			
Lower Arms			
Wrists			
Hands			
Knees			
Ankles			
Feet			
Back – Lower			
Ribs			
Calves			
Abdomen			
Forehead			
Head Shape			
Collarbone			
Profile			
Pelvis			
Backbone			

You don't need Amy's fashion savvy to tell you to accentuate the positive and change, minimize or ignore the negative, do you? (And I hope all your check marks aren't in the middle column. If you hate yourself that much, you need more than wardrobe counselling.)

So, as the doctor says to the patient, 'All right. You can get dressed now.' Please put on a couple of your favorite ensembles from your closet, and stand again before your three-way, full-length mirror. You've already decided that you like the way these outfits look on you. Now, based on your self-assessment can you analyze why?

If you're happy with what a particular outfit does for you, it's probably because it enhances something (you named it above) that you like about yourself, or minimizes something you're not crazy about in yourself. For example, Amy loves a dress she owns (in both a summer and a winter version) because it's got built-into-the-seams curves, which somehow make her straight-up-and-down figure seem like an hourglass. Her friend Rebecca loves nothing better than long, straight dresses. Why? Her weak point, she feels, is her legs, which are thick and straight. Yet her hips are slim. The long-line dresses show off what she's decided is appealing, while making what she doesn't like less noticeable.

There are no rules here. You must figure out what works best for you, and makes you happy. **But don't lie to yourself or make excuses you don't believe in. Be courageous.**

One last mirror suggestion: when you check out your outfit in front of your mirror before you leave the house, move, bend and turn a bit. Don't stand like a waxworks display. That way you'll see if the dress's wrap sash starts to come undone, or the seam of the seat of your pants starts to ride up. And you'll see yourself more as you really are – really the key to this exercise.

Cameras and Video Recorders

alk about seeing yourself as you really are, how about looking over whatever snapshots and videos have been taken of you recently? I know – the camera adds ten pounds and you never took a good picture. But study photos differently this time. Instead of hiding away the ones you hate and gazing with satisfaction at the ones you like, look more deeply. What is it that you really liked about that picture of you at your best friend's wedding? Do you love the way that little ribboned hat set off your large brown eyes? The way that red polka dot scarf brought a rosy glow to your skin? The way the long dark sleeves of your dress accentuated your pretty, expressive hands?

What is it that made you shriek in horror at the family Christmas video tapes? (Besides your mother-in-law's turkey?) Was it the sight of your belly bulging under your flowered silk dress? The cloud of frizz that you thought was your hairdo?

Always question the reasons for your reactions to your own image. If you can identify a reaction and name the problem that caused it, then you can solve it if you want to.

Incorporate the good looks into your daily wardrobe. Permanently drop the bad ones.

Use your camera, like your mirror, as an ally. It is a tool for accurate self-assessment, and can point the way to whatever change you would like to see in yourself. Here are a couple of exercises you can do with your Instamatic or video camera:

Exercise One

Get together with a friend, and have her take
pictures of you in different outfits. (Amy did this
with me and a Polaroid.) Talk, walk, move, sit, turn,
bend. Study the results. Again, decide what you like
and what you don't, and analyze why. Always ask
why. You can try this experiment another way
without an accomplice:

Exercise Two

At the next event when a camera is called for, have
someone take the usual casual, friendly snapshots or
videos. You will notice, (now that you will be
analyzing the results with a more enlightened,
concentrated purpose) that you are a bit more self-
conscious about how you look, how you behave, and
how you want to be seen. This is good. If you find
yourself feeling like a performer, remember you are
your own audience. **Turn your self-consciousness
into self-awareness**. This will help as you evaluate
the results of the photo session.

'Every eye is a mirror.' This is a line written by
Gloria Vanderbilt, (who Amy says is one of the most
sensational looking women she has ever seen). She is
a woman who has such self-awareness and assurance
that she never seems to think about her own

appearance. This complete sense of herself allows her to concentrate her attentions solely on whomever she is with, and that – not her considerable natural beauty – is the secret of her charm. For our purposes, we will extend Gloria's phrase to say that 'Every eye is also a camera'. Though the exercises you practiced at home may seem artificial and contrived, they are really a private enactment of what takes place every day, on the street, at work, at the grocery store, whether you like it or not! People – strangers, friends, and family – notice you wherever you go. We want you to feel good about that.

But if, despite help from mirrors and cameras, you still have trouble seeing yourself clearly and objectively, or if you need an aid to guide you from your household mirror out into the theater of life, here's a small suggestion: Imagine, as you're getting dressed in front of the mirror, and then as you go out and participate in the world, that there's a single, benevolent eye watching you. How do you look to this eye? You can think of it as a guardian angel, or an exterior part of your consciousness – whatever helps. This eye cares about you, but doesn't lie.

And here's some important parting thoughts from Amy that both of us have profited from:

What You've Been Told Are Your Defects May in Fact Be Your Strongest Points

*D*on't believe what you've been told by your family or your old boyfriends. Did it ever occur to you they may not always have your best interests at heart? 'Flap Ears', 'Skinny Minnie' and 'Stick' are all names Amy was called as she grew up. Well guess what? After years of hiding her ears, hating her weight and downplaying her height, Amy now accentuates those features. As a reedy five-foot-ten teenager she feared heels. To exaggerate her deviation from the norm seemed terrifying. Then her Uncle Ray pointed out that high heels would increase her height by a smaller percentage than they would on a petite girl. Ever since, Amy has gloried in the extra height heels allow. Go for it.

Make Your Imperfections Your Trademarks

*T*ruman Capote, who knew more about beautiful women than they know about themselves, invented a character in *Breakfast At Tiffany's* called Mag Wildwood. She was too tall, too clumsy, too flat-chested, and she stammered – but she was a drop-dead gorgeous, highly sought-after model. The secret of her extraordinary glamour? She exaggerated each of her shortcomings so that they became her charms.

Celebrities know how to exploit their physical irregularities. What would Barbra Streisand be without her nose, Esther Rantzen without her larger-than-life teeth, Paula Yates without – well, you get the idea. Dolly Parton *is* her white-trash glamour. (As Dolly says, 'It takes a lot of money to look this cheap!') Strangely enough, what you dislike in yourself may be exactly what others yearn for. I know an exercise instructor named Suzy who hates her pronounced jaw because her husband always makes fun of it. What I wouldn't give for a strong jaw line! It certainly never stopped Jacqueline Kennedy from being beautiful. As Francis Bacon wrote, 'There is no beauty without some strangeness in its proportions.'

It Is Seldom a Good Idea to Go Against the Grain and Force Yourself to Be the Opposite of What You Are

▼

*A*fter all, it never worked for Cinderella's ugly stepsisters: her dainty glass slipper still didn't fit. A straight-haired brunette seldom makes a good curly-haired blonde. Wonderbras and peplum waists will never turn a rail-thin waif into a Marilyn Monroe bombshell. An exotic-looking dark-skinned woman will rarely seem right dressed in a stuffy twinset and pearls. These attempts at an ego about-face are generally recipes for unhappiness. As the Greek philosopher Epictetus said, 'Know, first, who you are; and then dress accordingly.'

Change What You Can

*I*f you are truly miserable about certain aspects of yourself, if your posture, your thighs, your nose, your teeth are impossible to live with, don't pretend they're not a problem or decide there's nothing you can do. Don't be defeated. Go to an exercise specialist, a reputable (this is very important) plastic surgeon or cosmetic dentist. Go on a diet and stick with it. You can alter your fate. No one else can do that for you. (I've lost more than a stone since I started writing this book!)

Liberate Yourself from Those Wretched Little Rules That Strait-Jacket You

*S*uppress the noises made by that nasty little 'shouldn't' voice inside of you. It is the voice of self-loathing and fear. 'Redheads shouldn't wear pink', 'You're too skinny to wear black', 'You're too fat to wear stripes', 'You're too busty to wear knits', 'You shouldn't mix greens and pinks because they clash'. We believe that if you love a color you should wear it. And that style often lies in the reversal of these rules. A redhead can look fabulous in pink, and if you love your big bust line, why not show it off?

Abandon Your Fears, Your Denials, the Little Lies You Tell Yourself.

*B*e good to yourself. Be honest. Otherwise you are sleepwalking through life and will never be happy with the way you look, (or with anything else). The right clothes build up your self-confidence, the wrong clothes can have the opposite effect, points out author Judy James, a modelling school manager and lecturer in self-presentation. Lying to yourself is crippling. This is not a dress rehearsal. This is your life.

CHAPTER FIVE

Comfort vs. Style

or The Balancing Act (a Meditation)

*'It is only shallow people
who do not judge by
appearances'*
– OSCAR WILDE

*F*ROM A MODERN
perspective, the contrap-
tions that women have been
forced to wear in the name
of style – corsets, stays, steel
hoops, girdles – all seem like
torture devices. It's hard to think of
a single female garment that existed
between the Roman toga and the flapper's
shift that appears comfortable by contemporary
standards. But, strangely enough, women during all
these long centuries never really complained of being
uncomfortable. Diaries from the nineteenth century even
reveal that some women liked the sensation of being
tight-laced. Health issues aside, what does this tell us?

Comfort is as much a state of mind as a physical reality

Comfort is what a culture agrees upon as comfort. For example, up until the seventeenth century, nobody in the Western world even had upholstered furniture in their houses. Yet before padded furniture, nobody thought hard, upright wooden chairs were a problem.

When sixties feminists discarded their bras to celebrate their new freedom their gesture only made symbolic sense. Just ask any size 36D woman – Eve Pollard or any other one will tell you she'd be less comfortable braless than Steffi Graf would be playing tennis in platforms.

A male reporter once asked Amy what was the most comfortable garment ever designed, and she proposed the caftan. The next thing she knew he had gone into a closet and donned a caftan Amy's husband had brought back from Morocco years ago. And what do you think his assessment was? He felt uncomfortable, of course, because to him it felt like he was wearing a dress! (Just as well. He didn't really have the figure for it.)

Actually, I'm not comfortable in a caftan either, because I hate the sensation of my own bare skin rubbing

against itself – that's why I like trousers. I feel strangled
in a turtleneck; they make Amy feel secure. From all
these disparate viewpoints we have learned that as far
as comfort today goes, one woman's meat is another
woman's poison.

But comfort is also tied to **appropriateness**, the socially
accepted standards of the moment – that men (usually)
don't wear dresses, and that business women at work
don't wear visible black nipple-baring bras under their
white silk blouses. If you don't somehow resemble your
peers in the shop, office, or the classroom, you're
probably not going to be comfortable. If comfort were
all to do with clothes that don't restrict the freedom of
the body, we would be most comfortable with no clothes
on at all. But how comfortable are you stark naked? See
what we mean?

The good news is:

**Comfort and style are not necessarily contradictory
states of being. In fact they can be closely related**

Today most of our ideas about comfort in clothing come
from leisure and sports clothes. When women want to
'slip into something more comfortable' these days, they
don't mean a marabou-trimmed Jean Harlow satin

nightie. Most women reach for those worn leggings, a T-shirt, and a pair of trainers. I'm probably most comfortable in my old sweat pants, Nike Air Max and a soft flannel shirt. For Amy, it would be her white Fernando Sanchez bathrobe, and leopard mules. (This is why we both live in fear of video telephones.)

Let's examine, for a moment, the widely held conviction that jeans – that universal symbol of today's democratic style and the most successful single garment of the twentieth century – are a comfortable article of clothing. Oh, yeah? What about that tendency they have of biting your crotch? Ouch!! Or gapping at the waist, or pulling across your thighs. The fabric is rough (though appealingly durable), the seams are thick, lumpy, and heavy as canned ravioli. They're too warm for the summer, and too cool for the winter. Think about it. It's next to impossible to find a pair that fits well. And it's definitely not the best look on most women – though there may be some lovely exceptions. So what's the deal?

Our theory is that jeans fit the current image of what's carefree and casual. They are a secure choice: after all, everyone wears them, from movie stars to the kid at the car wash. They're democratic. So you feel *secure* in your garment – but not necessarily *comfortable*. Be conscious.

Jeans as comfortable wear are a myth we all bought!
Now understand, we're not saying 'Don't wear jeans'.
We're only pointing out they may not be as comfortable
a choice as you thought. And that many of our beliefs
are illusions.

Trainers are, in their way, more unattractive on the foot
than jeans are on the imperfect butt. Modern athletic
shoes are clumsy, goofy, graceless (aren't those names of
the Seven Dwarfs?) And they're deadly with a suit or
dress. So why do we cling to them? Ask anyone, and
they'll name comfort as the reason. Then why isn't every
foot in the nation shod in orthopedic shoes instead? The
answer is that Granny's podiatrically correct clod-
hoppers are linked in everyone's minds with infirmity,
while Nikes, Reeboks, etc. connote health and youth.

Here's another way of demonstrating the surprisingly
wide-ranging feelings about comfort: During Amy's
pregnancy, when her preoccupation with comfort was
heightened, she felt most at ease in a loose dress and
sandals. But her friend Martine detested the idea of a
dress, and instead lived for nine months in leggings and
smock-style blouses. When Amy tried out leggings, she
found they bound her knee, constricted her circulation,
and cut into her stomach. Comfort, girls, is relative –
relative to your own tastes, relative to the situation

you're in, and relative to the period in which you are living. So think about the roles you play in your life, and the clothes you need for them: try not to polarize your wardrobe into comfortable vs. stylish clothes – the jogging suit and sneakers vs. the itchy cocktail dress that cuts into your waist, the worn denims vs. the stiff business suit. As designer Betsy Gonzalez said, 'A woman should never wear anything she can't do the mambo in.'

What we are suggesting you aim for is an approach that doesn't make you uncomfortable, nor does it leave you inappropriately underdressed. To do this successfully means you must have an awareness of your own physical comfort as well as your lifestyle. It's too bad we don't all have the time, talent and liberty to re-invent clothes for ourselves. Designer Geoffrey Beene, who believes the male uniform of jacket and tie is obsolete, now only wears a jacket of his own devising. It is simply a man's suit jacket transformed by being made of a soft knit jersey fabric instead of a woven gabardine or flannel. 'It has the comfort of a cardigan, but the propriety of a suit jacket,' he explains. Comfort and style!

This is the kind of resolution of opposites we aim for. So, to review, when you think about your clothes and your wardrobe, remember that:

Comfort is partly a state of mind – not body – that can vary from one individual to another, one situation to another, one time period to another

Style does not necessarily contradict comfort – it can enhance it

A stylish woman is never uncomfortable in her clothes. She feels as good in her dinner suit as she does in her gardening clothes

You can probably find both comfort and style in your own closet

In the words of Yves St Laurent, 'Finding your own style is not easy, but once found brings complete happiness. It gives you self-confidence, always.' We aim to help you do that.

CHAPTER SIX

Weight a Minute!

*or A Waist Is
a Terrible
Thing to Mind*

*'There is nothing either
good or bad but thinking
makes it so'*

— SHAKESPEARE

I COULD BE
(and have been) called
'plump', 'rounded', 'pudgy',
and simply 'overweight'. What I
am is average. I am five foot four
(statistically average height for an
American woman) and, as I begin to write this
book, I weighed one hundred and forty-six pounds –
exactly average. (Now that is a sentence that takes
courage to write!) So, at average height and weight for
an American woman, why is it that I feel so much
shorter and fatter?

I always mean to lose weight. I exercise regularly and I haven't had a dessert (not even my own birthday cake) in the last two years. The fact is, sometimes I *am* ten pounds slimmer, but I'm still not happy because I long to be the eight stone I was at my college graduation. I am not alone. According to the Annals of Internal Medicine, most dieters manage to lose only ten per cent of the weight they hoped to – and, as most of us know from experience, even *that* doesn't stay off. The same report shows that one-third to two-thirds of dieters regain the weight within a year; just about all of it is back on within five years. Now, I'll grant you that Americans are weight-obsessed, but anorexia and bulimia are on the rise on this side of the Atlantic as well.

Anyway, the point is that for quite a few years I didn't make the best of myself because I was waiting for the magic to happen – I was waiting to be thin again.

WELL, I'M NOT WAITING ANY LONGER AND I DON'T THINK YOU SHOULD EITHER.

The fact is, recent surveys reveal that more than eighty per cent of us believe we are overweight, (and that includes adolescent girls and anorectics). Amy – who is five foot ten and whose weight barely gets out of the double digits – watches her eating as carefully as I

watch mine. Susie Orbach had it right when she wrote
Fat Is A Feminist Issue: We women are obsessed with
eating and weight loss. So I'm here to tell you once again
that your weight – whatever it is – is no excuse to put off
creating a wardrobe that is as flattering and comfortable
as possible.

I know that's hard. I refused to shop if I couldn't fit into
'my' old size, so I wore things that I could barely button
and that looked awful on me. Or I wore sweat pants and
a sloppy shirt to 'hide' my weight. Well, it didn't hide
anything, especially my lack of self-esteem and style.
Garmentos have taken advantage of our obsession and
shame over weight by their practice of 'downsizing':
enlarging size standards so that we can fool ourselves
into thinking we're a twelve. We haven't lost an ounce or
an inch, but our vanity is touched and our wallet is
emptied just because a maker put a size twelve label on
his size fourteens or sixteens.

Many of us fool ourselves by thinking that in just a week,
a month, or a year we'll be thin and perfect and that
until then it's useless to try to look good. Don't fall for
that kind of denial. Right now, today, your life is taking
place and – at whatever weight you are – there's no
excuse not to try to look as attractive as you can. *Carpe
diem*. Seize the day. There are several reasons to do it.

Looking Good – at Any Weight – Is Possible

I am not so optimistic or stupid as to say that a three-hundred-pound soprano can look just like Kate Moss. But we've seen Oprah Winfrey wax and wane and there wasn't a time when she didn't look well-groomed and put together. Her clothes fit properly, which did a lot to make her look attractive. She had – and has – her own style and panache, no matter what she tipped the scales at. And we all loved her for it.

Once, in India, I attended a business party with several male co-workers. The belle of the ball was a middle-aged Hindu woman in a sari. She was a dozen years older and easily outweighed me by fifty pounds, but there was something about her that kept the men entranced. She had charm and confidence. Later, when I asked one of the men about his reaction, he looked surprised and said, 'She was irresistible. She was so very self-assured and sensual.' He confided in me that he thought she was very sexy. And she was old enough to be his mother.

Now, I am not saying that it is easy in our society for a so-called overweight woman to exude self-confidence, but it can be done. Look at comedienne Dawn French; she doesn't try to hide her size but dresses with style and confidence and always looks terrific. And looking terrific makes you feel terrific. When you feel good you take better care of yourself.

Looking Bad Demoralizes You

*T*he surest way to gain more weight is to play ostrich, put your head in the sand and just hope the problem goes away. The other mistake is to give up. When I was in my sweat pants mode, even a glance at my reflection would make me feel so bad about myself that I would sit down and polish off a couple of chocolate bars. Looking bad is a kind of self-punishment that only increases your humiliation and self-hate. Right now, today, get dressed comfortably and attractively in clothes that fit you, whatever your size. Finally . . .

Dressing Well and Looking Good May Actually Motivate You to Lose Weight

*D*on't believe that if you collect a beautiful wardrobe in size fourteen you will be stuck there forever. When I dropped a size because of my exercise program, I didn't hesitate to have my trousers altered and go out and buy a few nice new things in my new size. What a triumph.

Please notice that I am not suggesting a diet program or some magic weight loss exercise and eating regime. I say live in the present, whatever weight you are. Dress to camouflage those parts you are least happy with and to emphasize those parts you like best. Also, remember that you are not alone. There have been so many diet books printed that if I merely weight-lifted all of the ones I've bought I'd be as slim as Amy or Kate Moss. Nowadays we are all so infected with the anti-fat virus that the thinnest adolescent girls complain about their imaginary fat thighs while otherwise contented, attractive matrons long to regain their adolescent bodies. We should look to Continental women who, when they reach a certain age, neither try to emulate teenagers nor give up and sink into an elastic-waisted skirt and an oversized man's shirt. They dress well and appropriately and I try to do the same. And one advantage of a bit of fat is that it does soften the facial features. As a famous French beauty (who had, with age, put on some weight but few wrinkles) said, 'It's either my face or my ass!' So I struggle to stay in my size, look good, and like who I am. (By the way, I have barely a wrinkle on my pudgy, over-forty face!)

CHAPTER SEVEN

Strategies

or Six Never-
Fail Fixes

'Our life is frittered away by detail . . . Simplify, simplify'

— HENRY DAVID THOREAU

O KAY, SO NOW you've assessed what you have in your closet and what you look like in your clothes, but maybe you're still not certain about how to put together a 'look'. Presented below are six never-fail fixes. One of them just may make sense for you.

Use a Single Color

*P*riscilla, a big, tall, Texas blonde wears virtually any silhouette, from a minidress to a formal suit – as long as the outfit is red. 'Valentine red makes me happy,' she explains. 'And I get my variety in wearing my skirts slim or full, or wearing trousers and sweaters any shape I want to. It's just all in red. It's become my trademark, in a way. All my friends give me red gifts. My little sister does the same with cotton-candy pink.'

This one-color strategy is especially common in the fashion world, though there the color of choice is most often black (a gathering of designers, models, and editors could be mistaken for a pallbearers' convention). Why black? Because almost all blacks go together – not to mention the fact that the day's stains and wrinkles seem to disappear, and that black is always slimming. Also, black has been perceived as chic since before Chanel invented the little black dress.

But remember that there is a complication in the one-color strategy: not all oranges are created equal. Nor is the one color that you have chosen always going to be available.

One reason why the monochrome look is most popular
with red, black, white, beige or navy is because these
colors are fashion perennials and almost always offered
each season. Even if a color is meant to be consistent, dye
lots change from bolt to bolt and season to season. Certain
colors are deemed to be 'in' by the garmentos one season
only to disappear by the next one. If you've settled on your
favorite shade, just be warned that color is sometimes
harder to match than to contrast or combine.

Stick with the Perennial Fashion Colors

As mentioned above, this is another color-based
fashion strategy. Use black, white, red, beige and
navy. You can build a wardrobe just on these colors and
add from the best of any new season's offering, secure in
the knowledge that they will mix well together.

Select a Single Silhouette and Stick with It

*T*his one is tricky, since we know all too well that silhouettes change faster than leaves in autumn. Mary, Amy's friend, is arrestingly chic at age eighty and has been wearing the same dress for decades. Boy does she look great in it. No, not just one dress, silly! A whole closet full of jewel-necked, long-sleeved, knee-length chemises that she sews herself, copied after one very costly original purchased way back in the mists of time. Amy's seen it in fluttering light silk in the summer, thick nubby tweed in the winter and it never ceases to impress. Mary not only found her style at an early age, but had the courage, savvy and spirit to stick with it.

A friend of mine bypasses retail establishments altogether. Tomboy casual yet well-groomed, Jan wears either jeans and cardigan sweaters she handknits, or suits made by her husband's tailor, 'always cut from the same pattern. And cheaper than lots of off-the-rack women's suits.'

Sophia Loren has her own version of this strategy. 'I like
classic clothes for day, but when I go out at night I like
fluffy evening dresses. When you walk in in one you feel
like you are conquering the world.' Well, it works for her.
I'd feel silly and self-conscious in a huge taffeta skirt.
But hey, she's got her (two) uniforms and I've got mine.

Stick with a Single Designer

*T*here are times when that rare miracle occurs. You
try on a dress or a suit and you know it was made
for you. It fits everywhere, it flatters, it feels good. You
want to wear it out of the shop and never take it off. You
want to sleep and shower in it. Who designed it? What's
on the label? Thank the maker. If you're lucky (and the
designer is good) it will be like coming home every time
you slip on his or her clothes.

Some actresses use this strategy. Patricia Hodge always
wears Jean Muir while Jodie Foster always attends the
Oscars in an outfit by Armani. And many designers only
wear their own creations, Vivienne Westwood and
Zandra Rhodes amongst them.

But buyer beware: With clothes pattern makers, fitting models, and producers changing as often as your underwear, and design teams large enough to fill a football stadium, consistency in a given label is rare and should be valued. When it's found, be faithful.

Stick with a Single Outfit in Every Color Available

*S*everal designers told us their most fashion savvy clients often purchase the same outfit in every color available, rather than buying all over the entire collection. The manager of Harrods's chic shoe boutique says that her most well-shod customers do the same with their favorite pumps or boots. I myself have identical pairs of terrific lace-up boots in black, brown and tan.

Dark Bottom, Colored Top

*A*s I mentioned in Chapter Three, I came up with a fairly simple solution for myself: Pearshaped, like most women, I feel most comfortable and look best in dark trousers or skirt and tights. But because head-to-toe black is too boring and severe for me, I add my neutral-toned jackets and sweaters, often with a white blouse under them. If your upper half is your better half, I add this suggestion of Eleanor Lambert, creator of the International Best-Dressed List: 'Save interesting details and colors for above the waist – people will notice your face first, not your hips.'

The single idea that rings through all these approaches is that simplicity and discipline are necessities. Very few women have the time, interest, money, talent and lifestyle to support a wardrobe that requires Imelda Marcos's closetful of shoes and a dedicated ladies' maid. Yet you may feel these suggestions threaten you. Examine your resistance. Where's the variety? You may wonder. Where's the excitement? Where's the un-expected? Not to mention, what will you do with all that extra junk you no longer wear?

If you do feel threatened, ask yourself: Is this what I want from my clothes – excitement, variety, thrills? Sadly, we've observed that for many women, what they really want in their lives appears only in their closet. My friend Lisa kept buying little cocktail dresses whenever she shopped. One day, she had what we call a moment of fashion enlightenment. 'I never go to cocktail parties,' she confessed. 'But I can't stop buying these dresses. I think I want to live the life I'm shopping for.' There can be fun, pleasure, and excitement in your closet, but it should be based on your reality. If you don't have a place to wear a dress you want to own, then change your life, not your wardrobe.

The unifying principle behind each of these strategies is what we call **The Rule Of One**. One color, one palette, one silhouette, one outfit . . . ONE STYLE!

A few other rules to remember as you 'try on' a style:

Accept that you can't be everything.
Letting go is a part of this process.

Accept that you can't have everything.
Even if you could afford to, it wouldn't help you to look better. And, in the words of comedian Steven Wright, 'If you *did* have everything, where would you put it?'

Pick the things you can live in most comfortably and happily.
Some things look good but don't feel good.
Others are the reverse. People tell me that I look good in red, and I can see that I do. But I don't feel comfortable in red. So I've given it up. Decide on the things that work best both ways. We all want to find the utopian place where comfort meets good looks.

CHAPTER EIGHT

Getting Help

*or Finding
a Fashion Guru*

'When the student is ready,
the Master appears'
— CHINESE PROVERB

*W*ARNING:
do not read this chapter
until you have completed one
through six! And, if you have
already found yourself in your
closet, skip this chapter altogether.
But, if you are more confused and
disheartened than before, this chapter may
provide relief. Do not read while driving, or operating
heavy machinery. Do not mix this chapter with
alcohol and do not read it while pregnant.

So, you went into your closet to find yourself and there was nobody home. Or, worse, it seemed like a crowded costume party that you weren't invited to. Or, worst of all, you realized that you hated yourself and that your clothes advertised it.

What to do? There's only a limited amount of direction that any guide book can give. At a certain point, when lost in the back alleys of Kathmandu, you need to give up on the map and ask for help. To quote a friend's favorite Spanish proverb: Ask and you shall find Rome. (Or maybe Paris, or LA, depending on how you want to dress!)

If at this point you still don't know how you want to dress, please do not feel as if you have failed, or that this book has failed you. Look at it this way: You have already got more in the way of enlightenment than you had bargained for. No wonder you never felt good in your clothes! There is no shame at this point in getting the help of a good mentor. Style is not about copying, it's about evolving, but we do often need help to evolve. As the beat writer Lew Welch put it, 'Somebody showed it to me and I found it by myself.' You still get full credit.

The trick, however, is getting the right help. Look for what we call the 'Recognition Phenomenon': Just as you may have met or read about someone able to articulate perfectly the thoughts that you have trouble expressing, so there may be someone who can point you toward the perfect clothing that you have unknowingly been seeking. This process should not involve a slavish submission to anyone. (Remember, I learned from Amy's example, but I never copied her style.) Rather, it's a revelation of self – not unlike good psychotherapy. This chapter outlines the six means of getting fashion assistance.

~ Finding a Friend to Help

~ Finding a Saleswoman You Can Trust

~ Finding a Personal Shopper

~ Finding a Clothes Shop with Clothing You Like

~ Finding a Stylist

~ Finding a Woman Whose Style You Admire, Observing and Imitating Her Style

Each can deliver up style enlightenment, but be aware that each is fraught with perils. If you've been through the steps already outlined and still need fashion help, try one (or more) of these alternatives:

Finding a Friend to Help

*N*ow, do we have to define 'friend' for you? We aren't talking about someone who's jealous, someone with whom you compete, someone who seems to sabotage your efforts at love, diets, professional success – even though she may purport to be your buddy. And don't do this with a blood relative. (*Especially* a sister – so much emotional baggage, there'll be no strength left to carry shopping bags!)

So who should it be? A woman whose opinion you respect, a woman who dresses well, someone whose style you admire. It is not necessary that she be physically similar to you – Amy is nearly my opposite – but it might help. What's important is that she have your best interest at heart, your trust, a generous spirit, and a good eye or gift for fashion. Many women would be complimented to be sought after for advice.

Once you've chosen someone, here are some guidelines
that you might want to keep in mind:

Suggest that your first shopping foray be only
exploratory – explain that you want to look and try on
but not buy. This takes the pressure off both of you. In
our experience, women buy together but they return
alone. (Did you feel that chill wind?) Don't get
overcome by your friend's thrill in the moment, or swept
up into her enthusiasm for spending your money.

The acid test is returning to the shop by yourself, trying
on your selections calmly, and seeing if you really have
struck gold. (By the way, most retailers will hold your
choices without even a deposit if they smell an
upcoming sale.)

But you may not have a friend with the time, taste
or temperament to help. Which brings us to the next
option.

Finding a Saleswoman You Can Trust

*R*emember: smiles, compliments and coaxing
words are not necessarily to be heeded from a
saleswoman who may be making a juicy commission
from your purchases. Any good saleswoman knows that
a passionate but regrettable one-purchase-stand is
worth less to her than a stable, long-term relationship.
But most saleswomen aren't good. Also, bear in mind
that while many saleswomen are motivated strictly by
finances, there are those few professionals who are in
the business because they love beautiful clothes. These
traits are not mutually exclusive. Use several criteria to
judge the real value of a sales assistant. Ask yourself
these questions.

► Does she exclaim 'This is you!' even though she's never laid eyes on you before? (And are you looking behind you to see if there's someone else for whom she's holding up the same outfit?)

► Is she dressed in a way that you admire or want to emulate?

► Is she helpful rather than pushy?

► Does she seem condescending and snooty or excessively complimentary and fawning?

► Did she at first ignore you when you wanted help?

► Does she guide you to an outfit that you feel wonderful in or does she put you in something that paralyzes you with doubt?

► Even though you set a price range, does she steer you to much more costly items?

Once again, the safeguard here is time. *Don't buy anything.* A useful, knowledgeable vendor can be a great help in formulating a wardrobe but, like any good relationship, it won't develop overnight. Come back and try on her selections later, preferably without her. Only then should you consider purchasing them. And, whatever you decide, try not to worry about what *she* thinks.

Finding a Personal Shopper

*M*any of the better department stores now employ personal shoppers who can help with everything from a single special Christmas gift to entire wardrobes. The Executive Suite at Harrods offers consultants who give expert advice at no extra charge and many other department stores offer a similar service. Unfortunately, you do not always get to select the shopper. Often he or she is assigned, and although you may request a change, you don't get to audition everybody. Personal shoppers are usually (but not always) paid on salary, not commission. It is not impolite to ask which way they are compensated. If you find one who can efficiently take you from department to department, who can help match shoes to stockings

and who respects and enhances your idea of yourself,
then you may have found a guiding light on your quest
for style. (And a tip may be appropriate if her service is
extremely helpful.)

Finding a Clothes Shop with Clothing You Like

*M*y friend Caroline Taylor, who lives in Bath,
found a shop across the street from her office
where almost everything suits her. Not surprisingly, the
shop owner is built a lot like Caroline and has her fair
coloring. Caroline has been shopping there for over a
year now, and says, 'Eighty per cent of my wardrobe
comes from that boutique.'

We're not all this lucky. Finding a shop where the
styles, the price tags and the variety are in line with
your needs is not easy, but often a small shop is less
confusing and more service-oriented than a retail giant.
First of all, the editing of every season's offerings has
already been done by the buyer. And your requests
and inquiries will be acted upon. Shops will often make
special orders for you and provide or recommend the
best place for alterations.

Finding a Stylist

A fashion stylist works for magazines, catalogues and advertisers, creating the look and mood of a model. The secret weapons of makeup artists, hairdressers, editors, designers and photographers, stylists are the unsung heroes and heroines of the fashion business. But they are certainly not unpaid.

Stylists don't usually work for the fashion consumer, but you may get lucky, for a price. How to find a stylist? Call an advertising agency in your town. Call or write to a department store and inquire about an ad or catalogue picture they ran that you liked. Did they use a stylist? Who? Write to a magazine (numbers and addresses are listed on the masthead) and find out the name of the stylist responsible for a spread you are especially attracted to. (But remember, there is always a difference between what works in a photograph and what looks good in real life.) Finally, all else fails, there is the strategy of imitation.

Finding a Woman Whose Style You Admire, Observing and Imitating Her Style

▼

*I*f you really are having trouble identifying how you'd like to look, and who you'd like to be, think of someone, dead or alive, famous or obscure, whose style and personality you admire. It could be Audrey Hepburn, Grace Kelly, Joanna Lumley or Cher; it could be your favorite aunt, or your fiercest competitor at work. (Amy says that Barbie was her major influence.) Look at her, learn from her, mimic her (but if it is someone you know, don't let her know what you're up to. She may be more irritated than flattered.)

It helps to choose a style role model who is the same general physical type as yourself. And remember, this is meant to be a stopgap technique, not a permanent solution. But as *homo sapiens* we do learn by emulation. Imitate a style until you feel comfortable and you make it your own.

CHAPTER NINE

Dress Rehearsal

or I Thought I Liked It When I Put It On

*'In the beginner's mind there
are many possibilities, but
in the expert's mind
there are few'*
– D.T. Suzuki

*O*KAY, BY NOW
you should have managed to
put together what we call a
core wardrobe. Based on your
meditations, your self-assessment, and
your fearless expedition into your closet,
you've come up with an edited wardrobe of your favorite
and most becoming pieces. So now it's time for a trial
run because you may find, as I did, that a few of your
selections still don't work.

What you need to look at now are the real-life wearability factors.

We've broken them down into five general categories:

1. **Comfort** **(Again!)**

2. **Cleanability**

3. **Practicality**

4. **Appropriateness**

5. **Fit**

To make this assessment easier for you, we have created an evaluation card that allows you to rate these factors for any one of your outfits quickly. We use the old 'one-to-ten' scale, with one being as uncomfortable as a Queen Elizabeth I costume (complete with neck ruff and wig) and ten being your old cotton nightie. Anything that comes in with a rating of five or below ought to be reassessed and – unless you love it more than life itself – perhaps put aside.

Simple Isn't Easy
EVALUATION CARD

OUTFIT

Category	Rating 1-10		
Comfort	☐	☐	**RETAIN**
Cleanability	☐	☐	◉
Practicality	☐	☐	**REJECT**
Appropriateness	☐	☐	◉
Fit	☐	☐	

How to use this evaluation form

Make a few photocopies and label each one at the top
with the outfit you will be wearing. At least twice during
the day (before lunch and when you take it off were
good for us) assess how you feel in your outfit. Now
average them. Anything that scores under a five on
average, or that scores less than a three in any single
category should probably be eliminated from your
wardrobe.

Comfort

*A*my defines an outfit as 'comfortable' when she can put it on and 'not ever have to think about it again until I take it off'. It's a definition that works for me. For instance, Amy has two fabulous bracelets that she often wears in the summer. Each one consists of what looks like a thousand tiny seashells. The noise and the weight of them around my wrists would drive me nuts. But Amy loves them and never gives them anything but an admiring thought. My friend Brenda, a Glaswegian, can't bear to wear anything made of wool against her hyper-sensitive skin, but I find wool not just comfortable but cozy. Because comfort, (as pointed out in Chapter Five) is in the psyche of the wearer, and not in the garment or a rule written in this book, we recommend that you 'road test' each of your selected outfits to ensure that you feel really good in them.

Cleanability

*Y*ou don't have to have a doctorate in Environ-
mental Science to know that the world is not a
kind place for white silk. If you have reduced your
wardrobe to a lean closet, you will be crippled,
impoverished, and left naked if your clothes are not
available to you because they are constantly at the
cleaners. Many factors affect a garment's ease of upkeep and cleanability. Whites, creams and pastels more
obviously show dirt, while dark colors attract lint.
Synthetics retain stains, but white silk will yellow over
time (and not just under the arms). If a garment spends
more time at the cleaners or in the clothes basket than
in your closet, it simply might not be workable. And, in
this category, we also mention for your consideration the
wrinkle-resistance factor. Some fabrics crease like an
accordion the moment they are put on. Aside from
natural linen, most don't look good wrinkled.

My editorial assistant Nancy read the draft of this book,
decided on a look, and went out and bought four white
cotton shirts – her favorite. But she found they spend
too much time waiting to be washed and ironed. She's
back to knits.

Practicality

*D*o these clothes function as they are meant to? If they have pockets (my clothes must) are they too high or too low for your hands? If there is a front vent do you need to keep your legs wrapped around each other like a garbage bag's twist tie in order not to show your crotch? (This is assuming you're not into Sharon Stone flashing.) The neck may be flatteringly high and stiff but are you breathing? And while the waist is attractively nipped do you end up feeling like the girl in the magician's act, sawed in half? Does the suit look lovely, but have you sweltering in the summer, yet freezing in the autumn? Is the blouse fab, but so fragile that it has to be constantly guarded against snags? Your clothes should move with you, not against you, as you conduct the ordinary business of your life. They can be fussy or plain, but as long as they have the practical function of covering you where you want to be covered and giving you mobility when you want to move, they should stay in your wardrobe. If not, be ruthless.

Appropriateness

*A*s we pointed out in chapter one, what's fine for a cocktail waitress in a pick-up bar may not do for teaching a classroom of seventh-grade boys (though they might not object). You may love that lush, full-length mink that cost you a bundle but – animal rights aside – wearing it to your job as a social worker may just alienate a few clients, not to mention your boss. Something you have may be appropriate for certain aspects of your life but not others. You may want to reserve a few dresses too dowdy for your job or your social life to wear to dinner at your in-laws' or to visit your niece's convent school.

Clothes don't make the woman, but they can unmake her at the job. I know a woman whose work is exemplary; she held a position as executive director of a major non-profit making foundation. When her annual appraisal was done, she received performance ratings of 'excellent' from all of the board members, but they did comment that her casual Sixties wardrobe 'lacked professionalism'. It affected her raise. She was, above all else, surprised. She had no idea anyone noticed. So, when we discuss appropriateness it is not only your own opinion that counts; it is also the approval in the eye of the beholder. You must be sensitive to the effect you create and the way you are perceived by those around you. If you decide to disregard opinion, as she did, know the cost.

Fit

*A*my's favorite old Hollywood publicity photo-graph shows a studio costume department's collection of dress dummies, each a different shape and size, and each labeled with a different star's name. On most of these figures, padding has been added here and there to reflect the changing contours of the leading ladies' bodies. Whatever their weight, those old-time stars' figures always looked alluring, thanks to the ingenious fits provided by clever costumers.

If you analyze a stylish woman – whether in a great old black and white movie or real life – you will notice something even more subtle than the quality of her clothes, and the ease with which she wears them. One of the crucial reasons that she seems to be so 'comfortable in her skin', as the French say, is that her clothes really fit well. I've often wondered how women who spend thousands on French couture clothes can possibly justify the expense (apart from the fact that the cost represents such a tiny fraction of their bank accounts). Well, I've spoken to some

and these best-dressed women will not hesitate to tell anyone who cares to listen that there is nothing like having
a jacket or gown fitted on them, custom-made to their
own measurements. Standardized sizes fit nobody,
except maybe some pattern-maker's dummy.

You're no dummy. Sizes are just an estimate. They
represent no physical, bodily reality, certainly not yours.
So we recommend wholeheartedly that everything you
buy or own, unless it is one of those stretch jobs that
adapts to the wearer's shape, should be altered to your
own individual dimensions by yourself, a friend, or a
professional. Many shops and department stores employ
seamstresses to make these alterations, (sometimes – but
not often enough – free of charge). They can also refer
you to a competent seamstress if none is available on the
premises. Dry cleaners usually offer a tailor or
seamstress service. It's expensive but worth it. One outfit
that fits well is better than three that fit badly.

By the way, this does not mean that you can buy any
old garment and have it changed to suit your figure
exactly. Often sleeves cannot be lengthened, there is no
seam allowance to let out, or a waist is simply too high
and cannot be dropped. **A garment should fit reasonably well even before you take it to be altered.** Amy
has too often had a garment that she thought she

couldn't live without altered and re-altered, only to find
that she never wore it because, try as she might to turn
her sow's ear into a silk purse, that perfect fit eluded her.

What's Next?

*W*ell, at last! After this trial run and your final
evaluation, you ought to feel pretty comfortable
with your selections. Remember back at the beginning
of this little book we promised that you could actually
make money in this process? Now is the time. Your
financial rewards are going to come from three different
sources, and you may get some spiritual benefits as well.

It is time to go back to the boxes and bags of rejects. Yes,
you finally have to let go. But with that nice wardrobe
you are living in, it doesn't hurt too much, does it? Divide
your rejected clothes into those that are good enough for
resale shops (these are listed in your local yellow pages),
those that could be sold in a car-boot sale or flea market,
and those that can be given to charity. You may be
amazed at how much cash you can generate from the first
two. I hesitantly brought in a few of the better designer
clothes I'd rejected because they, alas, were far too small
for me. Not only did the retail store snap them up, the
store's manager begged me to sell her the old suitcase I

had brought them in! As Linda, one of my neighbors who ran a sale with me, put it on our home-made sign: 'Our junk, your treasures'. I thought she had a lot of nerve, but you should have seen the women grabbing at those cotton jerseys!

Charities such as Oxfam or Sue Ryder will welcome the clothes you can't or do not wish to sell and either sell them in their shops or take them to places where they are desperately needed.

So you've done some good works and may even have netted a profit. This is the part you have been waiting for! You have a new fund of money. What should you do with it? How about going shopping?

Now, we are not giving you *carte blanche* to fill those dresser drawers all over again. If the point of all this was to keep you in the endless squirrel's cage of fashion, that's how you jump back on the carousel. That's not the point! Sure, I was tempted. There was a silk outfit on sale that had my name on it. But the silk suit didn't 'go' with anything else I had and it wasn't on my list of necessities. Maybe it's on yours. I tried it on – twice – but I walked away from it.

So, how do you shop from now on? Turn the page to see.

CHAPTER TEN

Shopping

or a

Dangerous

Game

> *'Those who want the fewest
> things are nearest to the
> Gods'*
>
> – SOCRATES

*W*E ALL
have confessions to make:
shopping confessions. The
most expensive mistake I ever
made, oh Lord, was a lavender
leather suit. Go ahead and laugh. I
deserve it. But I cried over that suit. It was as
soft as rose petals and had been marked down from an
obscene price to ninety-nine dollars. I did not have the
money, nor a place to wear the suit, nor the right
coloring to make it work. But I was desperate that day
and it was so exquisite and such an enormous bargain.
Seventy-five per cent off!

The sales girl told me it was great and she was right. It was great for her if she could sell it.

You know the rest. I got home. I felt the excitement ebb as the thrill of the hunt turned into buyer's remorse. I tried it on at home and realized I looked ridiculous. But I hoped I could fix that. If only I could find the right shoes, and maybe if I lost just a few pounds and changed my make-up. (Not to mention my height, my face and my lifestyle, as well as my attitude.) The lavender suit was never worn by me. I couldn't even find a friend to give it to. The only use I ever made of it was to hang it in a character's closet in my novel, *The First Wives Club*.

Linda Grady, the Florida friend of mine who owned a clothing store for many years, knows almost everything about shopping. And yet she tells me that sometimes even she opens her closet to find that Sybil, her alter ego, has been secretly shopping behind her back. She believes we all have a Sybil inside us forcing us to buy clothes that just won't work. But we both believe that Sybil can be reckoned with.

To avoid horrible mistakes, extra expenses, wasted time, and the ruination of all of the work that you have done to organize your closet and create a personal style, shopping must be controlled. Author Judy James puts it this way 'Avoid the negative inner voice when you go shopping.' Now, since these days shopping is seen as a leisure activity, this is going against every instinct we've got and every belief that is holy. The garmentos will hate us for telling you this. Too bad. I don't say it's easy but I do say it is possible to break the compulsive shopping habit. And it is impossible to have and keep a style if you are constantly tempted by random merchandise, 'bargains' and impulse buys.

If you are committed to your excellent new look and to maintaining it, here are nine shopping rules to live by:

1. **Don't Shop when You're Miserable**

2. **Know What You Are Looking For**

3. **Keep a 'Needs List'**

4. **Don't Shop Alone**

5. **Don't Shop with the Wrong People**

6. **Beware of Sales**

7. **Avoid Extremely Trendy Styles**

8. **Don't Be a Magpie**

9. **Don't Shop When You're Miserable**

In twelve-step programs like Alcoholics Anonymous, there is a well-known and often quoted acronym: HALT. It stands for 'Hungry, Angry, Lonely and Tired'. People are advised not to let themselves 'act out' when they are feeling any of the four. Overshoppers should follow the same guidelines. Too many women shop to alter their feelings instead of facing them. Last time you went shopping and came home – loaded with bulging shopping bags but still unsatisfied – were you seeking something other than another pair of midnight-blue stilettos? Maybe what you really needed was a massage or a pleasant sexual interlude with your partner. Or maybe you were just feeling anxious and guilty because you still haven't returned your mother's telephone call. Or maybe you were angry over the unfair criticism you got at work. The point is, take the time to figure out what's ailing you before you binge. (And remember: clothes shopping ranks second after gambling as the most expensive mood-altering addiction.) You will never achieve a personal style if you are using shopping as a stop-gap for self-knowledge or therapy.

If you find that you have been using shopping that way, and you can't stop, consider real therapy, deeper reflection on what is missing from your life, spiritual counseling, taking up a new hobby or (at the very least) shopping for something other than clothes.

Know What You Are Looking For

*R*andom shopping invites random purchases. You know what I mean: a scarf you adore but that doesn't work with anything you own, a dress you have no shoes for and that no coat will fit over. This is how binges begin. Deirdre Allinson, a friend in Cheshire, once bought a pair of aquamarine suede driving gloves (marked down to almost nothing!) and wound up condemned to buy a matching suit, handbag, shoes, etc. – purchases which led to the final splurge of a white raincoat lined in aqua silk! I am not making this up - a white raincoat in Cheshire!

On the other hand, my publicist in London, the svelte Karen Duffy, is such a controlled shopper that she can find the one perfect garment in a dreary thrift shop or jumble sale. Nobody can put together an outfit the way she can, and she rarely loses her head, even when tempted.

How can you emulate that? When you let impulse buying take over, remind yourself you are being controlled by the evil garmentos, the stores, advertising, not to mention your own angst. If true personal style is self-expression through dress, then, like any artistic form, it is achieved by discipline, control, and balance. So when there is a lack in your wardrobe – a fabulous little black shift that needs to be replaced, a need for a new pair of warm trousers, or when there is a change in the weather that mandates a heavier (or lighter) coat, it is important for you to define that need before you seek to fulfill it. Smart girls know this. As model Veronica Webb said, 'I never go into the shops without knowing what I'm looking for. Otherwise one could go mad.' Shopping should be done not as a sport but with a specific goal in mind. Goals we approve of as specific and legitimate include:

Upgrading an Item that is Shoddy

Nothing replaces quality. A well-made garment cut from fine cloth does not look like a cheap one, and there is no way to fake good crafts-manship and superior materials. Follow the dictum of Amy's friend Babs, a retired fashion editor who says, 'Buy less, and buy the best'. By 'the best', we mean the best you can reasonably afford. Remember, if the choice is between six cheap and nasty suits and three good ones, you're better off with the latter. Amy's friend Joanne, for her first well-paying job after graduating from Harvard Law School, spent all her graduation gift money on three Chanel suits and nothing else. She wore them over and over again. They looked great, and so did she.

Adding a Basic that is Missing from Your Closet

When I went through the closet experience, I realized I was the victim of a strange phenomenon: I had twenty-five jackets and shirts that looked pretty good but virtually nothing to wear on the bottom! No wonder my closet was full but I didn't have a thing to wear! This realization only came about because of the *Simple Isn't Easy* approach, but once I noticed the pattern I knew the reason for it. I like the upper half of my body and I enjoy shopping for it. I can't say the same about my hips and thighs. But, after my realization, I also knew why I had such a hard time putting myself together. I simply didn't have any whole outfits. I was justified in going out and buying several pairs of trousers and a dress-up skirt. And it was interesting that – given my new knowledge – I still found myself drawn to blouses, jackets and sweaters. I had to force myself to concentrate on the items that I needed, rather than the items I wanted to buy. So, shopping for a missing necessary item is always legitimate.

Replacing a Proven Piece

Amy practically lives in black turtleneck
sweaters on winter weekends, but none of the
ones she owned ever seemed just right (the neck
was too loose, the wool was too itchy, or the
sleeves were too short). So, last year, she finally
got rid of the inadequate ones and replaced them
with a single, perfect black cashmere turtleneck
(which cost as much as all the others added
together!) If you have a useful item in your
wardrobe and you can afford to upgrade it,
that's the way to spend your shopping money.

With a leaner, more frequently used wardrobe comes a
new problem: pieces that you love will eventually wear
out. Heartbreak! A friend of ours voiced this complaint:
'After I sorted through my stuff, I did find the things
that looked great on me, but they were things I always
postponed wearing because I didn't want to spoil them!'
Are you a secret hoarder? Would you wear a rumpled
old cardigan and 'save' the attractive one 'for good'?
Don't do it! I know it's a hard habit to break. But
remember this is no dress rehearsal. This is your life!
And if that's not enough, remember the story of my
grandmother: whenever she was given a present she

particularly liked, she put it away 'for later'. After her
early death, her other grandchildren and I had to go
through closets and drawers full of beautiful things
Nana had kept 'for later'. We cried. (Hey, you, blot that
teardrop – it's time to wear things out and move on.)

Accept, then, that with the *Simple Isn't Easy* approach
all the clothes in your closet should eventually be good
ones and they are there to be enjoyed and worn out – in
both senses of the words! But we do have a tip for you:
When we find something that we adore and that we
know will continue to work for us, Amy and I stockpile
them: I have more than a dozen pairs of a matt olive
green tights that I wear with the same color boots. (I'll
never find either again!) And Amy has two pairs of
patent leather, low-heeled 'rain boots'. They don't make
them any more, and she wishes she had a third pair.
But, despite care and stockpiling, clothing will wear out.
That means that legitimate shopping for replacements
will happen. Just don't allow yourself to become
distracted and replace that smart navy woolen dress
with a floor-length magenta satin evening dress! (Not
unless you're planning to change your whole look and
your whole life to become a torch singer!)

Keep a 'Needs List'

*D*o rework a line from P. J. O'Rourke, going into a department store with a Gold Card and no objective is as dangerous a combination for a woman as car keys and a six-pack are for a teenage boy. So, after the closet clean out, I began to keep a needs list: things I was certain I needed and would wear. At one time last season my needs list looked like this:

- ▶ A black tropical-weight wool jacket (double-breasted?)

- ▶ Black silk trousers

- ▶ Brown leather shoulderbag (to match brown coat)

- ▶ Good-looking rubber boots (impossible to find!)

I found that it's helpful to have an idea of the style and color of a needed garment, but you may not be able to find exactly what you want and then the trade-offs begin. I also find it helpful to carry a swatch or some threads from the clothes in the main colors I want to match. (You can even tape them to the inside cover of this book.) But what you must not do is buy stuff not on your list.

So what happens if you see a fabulous sweater in just
the right color that would really be great with every pair
of jeans and trousers that you own? Plus it's marked
down to half price. You're going to hate me for this, but
I say forget about it. In your heart you know that three
times out of four you bring it home and it doesn't match
your trousers, or you add it to your pile of sweaters and
only wear it once a year. The point is you already have a
sweater or two or three (or a dozen if you haven't been
following instructions) that does the job nicely. And if
you don't, then the sweater ought to be on your needs
list already. Right?

In case of absolute emergency, when you see something
so perfect, so wonderful, such a good buy, such a life-
changer that you feel you'll die without it . . . don't buy
it. But you *can* put it on hold. It's a compromise. Insist
on a cool-down period. Reread this book, sleep on it, go
back and look at your spare but fabulous closet and ask
yourself if you really need it. Then determine what you
will give away if you do get the item.

If, after all of that, you buy the thing, Amy and I hope it
works for you. We've done the best we can.

Don't Shop Alone

*T*his rule may be broken by certain people – Amy regularly shops alone. But no one should shop alone when bored, depressed, recently fired or newly estranged from a husband. (Or right after leaving a shrink's office.) It's like that old rule for grocery shopping: don't shop when you're hungry.

While researching *Fashionably Late*, I noticed that the compulsive shoppers were those who showed up at the mall day after day and – like serious drinkers – they always shopped alone.

Don't Shop with the Wrong People

*W*e know this sounds like something your mother told you, but if she did tell you this, it was one of the few times she was right. I love my girlfriend Melody, but she's not a good influence when we're shopping. She's too kind to tell me I look lousy in something when I do and she wants an excuse to spend money so she pushes me to spend mine. Friends like Melody are best to visit museums with – museums that don't have gift shops!

And don't shop with one of those 'friends' who tells you how bad you always look in trousers, or 'helps' you by suggesting a diet that worked for her. We've all been demoralized by fluorescent bulbs in scary clinical white dressing rooms. We don't need help from 'friends' who habitually put us in an even more unflattering light!

There are also those who are loving friends but just don't have a sense of style. They don't even recognize style when they see it. As the Chinese poet Lin-Chi put it:

> When you meet a master swordsman,
> show him your sword.
> When you meet a man who is not a poet,
> do not show him your poem.

Beware of Sales

I interviewed a vice president of a major fashion department store who explained to me how most sales worked. 'We will lower prices on some things,' he said, 'but the really good stuff usually sells before the sale at full price.' By the end of the season – while you can get a great buy – there's often a reason why the stuff is so marked down.

Again, if you know that you need a navy coat and you have a pretty good idea of what it ought to look like, there's no reason not to wait until the January sales. But, because you are no longer impulse buying, and because you now have a clearer idea and a more discerning judgment about what you want, you may realize that you can only get it at the beginning of the season when the selection is widest. And because you are buying less, the sales savings may be immaterial.

Avoid Extremely Trendy Styles

*I*f you're buying just to jump on this season's band-wagon it's a mistake – unless the purchase is fairly disposable, like a tight fitting T-shirt or body in this season's newest color. You may, on the other hand, adopt some trends which you know work for you and turn them into your own classics, regardless of what's on the catwalks or in the magazines. Through the last drop in hemlines, both Amy and I continued to wear short skirts, secure in the knowledge that this was our favorite and most flattering hem length. Amy says, 'Long skirts weigh me down and short skirts – because they free the legs – give me more mobility. Besides, on both men and women, legs are my favorite part of the body.'

As a fashion writer, Amy is often asked by women outside the industry, 'Will my corset bustier/bell-bottoms/platform shoes/shoulder-padded jacket still be in style next year?' Amy's answer to such questions is, 'If you feel you look good in it, and you love it, wear it. And if you don't, discard it.'

Don't Be a Magpie

A magpie zooms in indiscriminately on every shiny little gimcrack that catches its eye, then schlepps the stuff back to its nest. Whether it's real gold or tin-foil, the magpie brings it back home. Amy and I want you – unlike the magpie – to be able to see past surfaces and into essences. This may take a little concentration, but it's not really different from being able to tell that one brand of fudge ripple ice cream has oozier chocolate veins than another. Don't be seduced by a cheaply made nightgown with dazzling gold lamé inserts, shiny bows, and frou-frou lace trim while passing up a quieter, simpler – but beautifully bias cut – gown with less of what the garmentos call 'hanger appeal'.

As an exercise, look in a large department store and see
if you can distinguish the differences between a lower-
priced and a higher-priced handbag of similar design.
Or the difference between a well-made, expensive belt
and a knock-off of it. A fleeting glance will reveal only
similarities, but if you linger to touch, smell (don't
insert in nostrils!), and handle the weight of both belts,
they may begin to vary considerably. If you are not
buying hastily, in a giddy, altered state of mind, you're a
lot less likely to be fooled by inferior, gimmicky
merchandise which will only (like a handsome but
heartless boyfriend) disappoint you in the end. If you're
thinking that you can't afford to buy the better version,
and you have no choice but to get the imitation,
remember one of our few rules: that you should buy the
best but buy less. And maybe, if you can't get a really
good one, you should pass up the purchase entirely.

CHAPTER ELEVEN

Accessories
After the Fact

or Finishing
Touches

'Everything should be made as simple as possible, and no simpler'

– ALBERT EINSTEIN

*O*NE OF MY favorite cartoons shows a fashionable woman, illustrated in the over-the-top style of True Romance comics, saying, 'I'm so grateful for my God-given ability to accessorize.' Silly as she may seem, the knack of putting the right finishing touches on an outfit is a rare and enviable gift. Accessory adeptness is not a question of matching the belt to the bag to the shoes to the nail polish. That approach is as hopeless as trying to create a master-piece with a paint-by-numbers kit.

Like good painting, accessory adeptness is about adding, eliminating, balancing, contrasting, and arranging textures, colors, shapes and proportions. And it can make the difference between a ho-hum outfit and a knock-out. If you feel you, too, have a 'God-given ability' then, like some of the world's chicest women, you might want to go to accessory extremes and make an indelible style statement.

In the Jazz Age, the eccentric shipping heiress Nancy Cunard startled her contemporaries with her ivory bracelets, stacked from wrist to elbow. She could have afforded diamonds, but ivory was more original (and not endangered back then). Oil heiress Millicent Rogers covered herself in overscale Native American-style turquoise and silver jewelry, some pieces of her own design.

If, like me, your accessorizing skills are more modest, or your job requires conservative dress, you are better off playing it down, and adorning yourself with, at most, one or two trademark pieces. I habitually wear a sumptuous scarf draped across my shoulders. Amy totes a fabulous polka-dot Gene Meyer handbag almost everywhere she goes. Lucinda Chambers, senior fashion

stylist at *Vogue*, advises to 'Start plain and simple, add
to it by wearing a great bag, could be second-hand
could be quite mad, but you have to love it. The same
goes for a pair of shoes. Remember to keep it simple if
you are not sure.'

Although just about anything from a tiara to a paper
bag can be considered part of your outfit, there are
usually ten basics to consider:

- Shoes

- Handbags and Shoulderbags

- Jewelry

- Scarves

- Hats

- Sleepwear and Loungewear

- Briefcases

- Glasses

- Hosiery

- Coats

Shoes

*S*tilettos, pumps, slingbacks, platforms, clogs,
boots! The sight, smell, and feel of a new pair of
shoes excite a stylish woman's senses more than a
parure of jewelry or a pan of fresh brownies. No doubt
about it, women are obsessed with shoes. They boast
about the number they own, one-upping each other like
old guys with their fish stories. Most women have an
unlimited appetite for shoes. Although I abhorred
Imelda Marcos's politics, I understood her shoe closet.
For my money, shoes are the Number One Most
Important Accessory. Like a rotten egg whipped into a
soufflé, badly made or poorly cared-for shoes degrade
the rest of your look, no matter how elegant or costly. Of
all articles of clothing, shoes are probably the most
accurate index of taste. Amy's hairstylist says he
surreptitiously studies a new client's shoes as a way of
gauging her character.

No two pairs of feet are built alike, and even your own
two feet are not identical. Yet sizes are standardized, as
if one size eight were the twin of every other (and wider
and narrower widths are now rarer than unicorns –
that's why women develop corns!). In the old, pre-mass
production days, shoes were designed, as clothing was,

on the body of the individual who wore them. Well, at least you can alter your dresses – but almost nothing can be done about shoes that don't fit. So let's get to it! *Simple Isn't Easy* techniques strike again! Toss out of your closet those shoes that were supposed to 'give' or 'stretch'. They almost never do – or not enough anyway. (Shoemakers can sometimes stretch the width of a shoe, but never the length. And when you request a stretch, make sure to ask for a 'toe box' stretch too, to create as much extra space as possible.) If you absolutely can't resist a marked-down pair of shoes in the wrong size, buy too large – never too small. You can insert insole cushions to reduce them somewhat.

As always, when a difficult question is raised, we find an answer in one of our hallowed *Simple Isn't Easy* precepts.

Find the shoe label that fits your foot best and stick with it - be a shoe loyalist. The right shoes feel good from the start, without any breaking in period.

Shoe-mania can easily get out of control. (Look at Imelda.) Remember then that there is a definite disadvantage to having too many pairs. The difficulty is that both trousers and skirts will each have their own ideal shoe height and shape. A pair of trousers that look terrific with a chunky two-inch heel will look lousy with a spindly one-inch one. It can be a lot of extra trouble keeping track of which shoes go with which hem lengths. Amy solves this problem by having one pair of shoes designated for each of her dresses. (But then she does have two walk-in closets. She claims she reserves one pair of shoes for walking into her walk-in closet!) My way of keeping it simple is to have all of my slacks hemmed for two-and-a-half-inch stacked heels. And I wear my skirts with three-inch pumps. Another easy solution for trousers that Amy proposes is to wear them with ankle-high boots. (Toned-in hosiery is then less of a problem . . . it's not visible.)

Finally, bear in mind this astute advice from Parisian shoe designer Christian Louboutin: 'Shoes are not really about fashion. What matters is not whether high or low heels are "in", but that a woman walks and moves beautifully and gracefully in them.'

Handbags and Shoulderbags

Quality over quantity, as always, is the best *Simple Isn't Easy* principle for bags. Handbag designer Marcia Sherrill gives the following sound (and not necessarily self-interested) advice: 'A bag should be an

enduring thing,' she says. 'Buy something tried and
true, devoid of a lot of gimmicks, something that can
see you through as many occasions as possible, and that
you can wear absolutely every day. Stay away from
suede and fabrics – they don't wear as well as leather. A
good rule of thumb: a bag should cost about the same
amount as what you would normally spend on one
outfit. Don't scrimp! Bags are as telling as shoes.'

It helps to define what bag works best for your needs,
and your wardrobe. For day and evening I stick with a
shoulderbag because I need to have my hands free. This
may be important to you too (Coco Chanel designed the
first shoulder strap bags to free women's arms). Amy
prefers structured bags with a handle rather than a
shoulder strap because her clothes tend to have sharp,
precise lines. She doesn't like shoulder straps because
they mar the drape. Maria, a writer friend who has had
a back problem, likes stylish backpacks because they
give the arms more freedom – and they complement her
sporty clothing. None of us have time to change our bag
daily to match our changing outfits. (By the way,
whatever style you pick, ruthlessly edit the contents of
your bag so that it does not resemble a badly sorted
recycling bin.)

Jewelry

*A*my and I both agree that when it comes to jewelry, forego the puny little 'genuine' pieces (tiny butterflies on a chain, microscopic diamond chips in a weeny heart, suitable for a sweet sixteener.) We've got not a thing against the real goods, mind you, just the namby-pamby nonsense that does nothing for anybody except the jewelry retailer. (An insider's secret: those minuscule gold nothings have the highest markup of all and have virtually no resale value.) So, if you must have gold, choose one real gold something over lots of gold nothings – even if you have to wait to accumulate the cash for it. Or, instead, put your money on an important costume piece. If you're worried about investment, first of all you are buying jewelry for the wrong reason and, secondly, costume pieces are breaking auction records these days. (Amy's friend, the costume jewelry designer Mish, says that his work 'imitates nothing – it's genuine Mish!'.)

Overloaded and understated are both good looks. Just make sure you have the panache to pull off the former and the restrained elegance to carry off the latter. Coco Chanel wore tons of necklaces – mixing faux with real in a revolutionary way. And Helena Rubinstein – all of her piled gems were the real thing, dear – mixed precious and semi-precious, colored stones (her passion), baroque pearls, and diamonds. The fact that she was barely five feet tall did not stop her from thinking 'the bigger the better!' Great, though maybe not for the laundromat or the average working girl!

The safest and easiest jewelry to wear is the brooch. A well-designed pin adds a touch of sparkle to a lapel or neckline without a lot of hassle. I wear a (fake) gold cameo-shaped pin almost daily. It's Medusa's head and as you know, she had the power to turn men to stone. I've needed that in business at times! It's my gold badge of courage.

As I mentioned, Amy often wears two bracelets – one on each wrist. They complement her long, muscular arms and tinkle and glisten in a seductive, subtle way. But Amy doesn't teach piano and isn't a court stenographer. If you are, be aware that bracelets can be noisy and distracting at business meetings or presentations.

Earrings are my private addiction. I'm always searching for the perfect pair. And they don't take up much room. But as a *Simple Isn't Easy* philosophy, don't let mistakes clutter up your jewelry box. Toss out, give away, sell, or trim your Christmas tree with all the baubles in your drawer that you have not worn in the last millennium.

Scarves

*F*or color, fantasy and drama, or neatly tailored chic, the scarf is the most versatile of all accessories. These basic rectangles or squares of cloth are the simplest unit of clothing, yet because they come to life only through the wearer's creativity, they are also the most intimidating. If you'd love the color and panache of scarves but can't get the knack of wearing them, I recommend taking a lesson in how to tie them from a more expert friend. (Try a French acquaintance - they're all born with a scarf-tying gene, and they wear them as nonchalantly as their eyelashes.) There are instructional books available, though most overwhelm me with difficult diagrams and really weird knot suggestions. Pick just a few styles – and ignore the origami-like instruction on how to build a replica of the Eiffel Tower with your scarf. Finally, whatever you do, don't tie that silken explosion of color into a boy-scout neckerchief. You'd be better off giving up on the whole scarf idea.

Hats

*Y*our great grandmother only took them off for her
bath, but when do *you* put them on? Hats can do
more wonders for your face than the most deftly applied
cosmetics, but how not to feel like a goon in one?
Weddings, church services, Ascot – sadly, there are few,
if any, other occasions that call for them anymore. And
it's even worse in the US. For the women of the last
century, and the first half of this one, hats had the same
allure that shoes now hold for us. But sixties bouffant
hairdos, followed by the decade's relaxing of mores,
brought about this dreadful hat obsolescence. All those
lovely gestures and rituals, all those glorious possibilities
for shape, color and trimming, all the intrigue and
flirtation of the veil – gone, gone, gone! Except, of
course, in the Royal Family

If you're a hat fancier – like Molly Parkin – and if
you've got a head for millinery, all is not lost. Amy is
partial to headgear herself – neat, pillboxish affairs, or
berets, (never broad-brimmed picture hats or sweet
country-girl confections) and she has the nerve and style
to wear them. But for the rest of us there are at least
two (seasonal) excuses to keep hats on our heads,
without looking inappropriate: *winter* and *summer*. One

for warmth (you lose up to eighty per cent of your body heat through your bare head) and the other for sun protection. But, whatever your excuse, if you feel foolish in a hat, don't wear it. It must be worn with security and confidence, even indifference. (This is how a stylish woman wears all her clothes.) I'll never forget the sun hat I bought in Martinique – expensive straw with a black grosgrain band. As I walked across the hotel patio to my chaise, a woman rushed up to me and breathlessly asked where I'd got the hat. I knew I had a hit. (And I told her I didn't remember!)

Sleepwear and Loungewear

*T*here are some of us who look lovely by day and fall completely apart at night. Oh, I know you wouldn't do that, but just in case, I want to point out that it is very easy to create an attractive, around-the-house uniform. I have three pairs of white cotton pajamas for sleepwear and, over time, they have become soft and delightful. Meanwhile, I also have my beloved sweats – a collection of nice looking and nice fitting soft clothes that I wear at home.

My friend Gillian is a master at the creation of a
comfortable at-home uniform. A stunning blonde, she
admitted that she has spent close to five hundred
pounds on five of the exact same black DKNY caftans
that she slips on when she comes home from work. Just
think: her husband has never seen her in a ratty old
robe. You may not be able to afford to spend that much,
but you don't have to. My pajamas were mail order, and
I got my sweats at clearance sales.

Briefcases

*D*on't be one of the boys. Unless you're a female
cross-dresser (and then you're reading the wrong
book, honey) pass up the really masculine attaché case
for a stylish, neat tote bag or oversized handbag. Those
hard-edged attachés belong in the same circle of fashion
purgatory as that dated, female yuppie suit-with-
sneakers look. And they hurt when they bump your leg.

Glasses

*W*hat do Elton John and Sophia Loren have in common with Magenta Devine? Signature eyewear. Great spectacles or sunglasses are a fantastic look-maker, and a marvelous cover-up on days when you are tired, or just couldn't deal with full eye makeup. If a frame works wonders on you, consider your glasses as a cosmetic, no matter how much of a medical necessity they actually are. Have duplicates made in case the frames are discontinued, and if they are, search for an approximate replica.

Hosiery

*T*he sheerest, smoothest, silkiest tights always look the most graceful – and always cost more than supermarket brands, which tend to appear blotchy and grainy against the skin. So buy the best you can afford. All brands, and all price levels of tights snag, tear, and run with maddening frequency. Good-looking run-free hosiery is one of those commodities (like petrol-free cars) for which the technology probably exists, but if it was introduced would kill off whole industries. Until durable sheer stockings see the light of day, here are some tips for stylish legs:

The greater the ratio of Lycra to nylon, the better looking and the longer-lasting the stocking.

Reinforced toes prolong the life of delicate tights. But please don't wear with open or low-cut shoes because they compete with the design. (You already knew that, right?)

Flesh-colored stockings used to have a bad fashion rep, but good manufacturers make them now in tones that blend as beautifully into the skin as a good make-up base. They can make your legs look as smooth as a store mannequin's, and they're often prettier than ivory-colored stockings (which can get Alice-in-Wonderlandy). Plus you don't have to worry about matching legs to shoe or dress. And should you get a run in the line of duty it won't show as much.

Black opaque tights, in either a shiny or matte finish, are very long-lasting, and perennially stylish (they're a favorite of fashion folk). They're warm, slimming, and superb with black suede shoes or boots. Sheer black is also often an attractive choice.

When you find the tights that function best for you, buy stacks at a time and store them. And buy at sales. Most stores run annual specials.

But if you think tights were invented only for bank robbers' masks, then stay in trousers or long skirts. Please throw out hosiery with pulls or snags, even if there are no runs. They make your legs look diseased. If you want to get more life out of them, wear them under trousers.

Suspenders and stockings do have the practical advantage of allowing one snagged leg to be replaced at a time, but who can be bothered with the hardware? In another lifetime I'll be the kind of girl who wears them.

Well, that about wraps up the accessory subject, except for wraps themselves.

Coats

*C*oats are more than an accessory since when you are wearing one it is a total look. And in the winter, it is what you are most seen in. But, all too often, women seem to forget that the coat and what's under it ought to bear some relationship to one another. You know the disjointed look I mean – a frilly formal dress worn with a ski jacket. Well, perhaps I'm exaggerating, but you get the point.

Amy loves the idea of color in winter coats – so cheering on bleak days. For ten years she's worn the same long, lilac, shawl-collared swing coat in mohair – fantastic with black accessories. I keep to neutrals, but then for me **simple isn't easy**. Some hints to help with coats:

* Be sure they slip easily over suit jackets, dresses, bulky sweaters.

* Beware of piling up shoulder pads on top of shoulder pads – you'll turn into a no-neck monster.

* Hems of skirts or dresses should not peek out below hems of coats, if it can be helped.

* At night and for parties, if you don't have a coat long enough to cover a full-length evening gown, wear a warm wrap or stole instead.

* The line of a beautiful coat will be destroyed if you sling your bag's shoulder strap over it diagonally, from shoulder to hip.

* Please save anoraks or ski jackets for out-doorsy wear. Get a real tailored coat for city wear. Remember the rule of appropriateness.

You also won't be surprised to hear that I have a pair of gloves for each coat, which I stuff in the pockets, and a wool challis scarf for each one. The scarf is not only warm, it can cover a neckline where a blouse collar is popping out or a blazer makes an inconvenient bulge. The scarves also relieve some of the dullness of my purposely neutral colored coats. Whichever approach you choose, bright or neutral colors, or whichever one you create for yourself, remember that the most carefully orchestrated look can be ruined by a coat that is only an afterthought.

CHAPTER TWELVE

Maintaining the Lean Closet

or Keeping It Down

*'Darling, you don't need
that. You have enough
already'*

– HALSTON

WHEN I WAS
very young (and then not so
young) I couldn't go to sleep at
night unless the closet door was
completely closed. It didn't matter
how many times the light was turned
on, the sliding door opened, the inoffensive
contents revealed to me – I knew that powerful monsters
lurked there. (Luckily, they weren't powerful enough to
get out unless the door was left opened.)

In a sense, even then I knew. As revealed earlier, most of us do have monstrosities hanging in our closets, and the condition of those closets themselves are pretty horrifying. You know what I mean: one garment flung over another; clothes swathed like Marley's Ghost in wretched and totally impenetrable dry-cleaner poly-ethylene; heaps of unidentifiable garments that have slid to the floor. Not to mention how you have broken *Mommie Dearest* Joan Crawford's sacred rule: no wire hangers!

A well-organized closet is not just a comfort and a useful tool to a woman. It is a necessity. And it is also a reward for all of the work you have done. A closet's condition somehow corresponds with your mental state. How much more serene we feel when we know that behind closed doors all is clean, clear and orderly. Closet fantasies are intriguing: Amy has a recurrent dream that she opens her closet doors and, to her great delight, discovers within it extra space, wonderful new clothes, and organization. And whenever I feel overwhelmed, confused or bogged down, I straighten out my (already neat) closets.

Interestingly, designers and retailers have begun to understand and exploit the seduction of a beautifully organized closet. The closet rebuilding and organizing industry has developed virtually overnight into a booming business. Designer Donna Karan understood the lure of a well-coordinated closet when, one season, she actually sold her clothes from a wardrobe. As an assistant explained: 'Putting them in a closet is part of Donna's philosophy . . . the closet is a natural setting for the contemporary woman's lifestyle.' For you to look good, your closet has got to look good.

This doesn't mean spending a fortune on built-ins or cedar paneling or wire basket holders. The greatest luxuries in any closet are not its fittings but its contents and space. And now, with your new, lean wardrobe, your closet should have all the space you need. But using the space well is an acquired skill, and I did get some tips from the experts. Just as artfully displayed clothing in a shop or boutique helps you to select and purchase it, beautifully displayed clothing in your own closet will help you to dress better each day. A small investment in closet fixtures will pay big dividends in savings. You'll have fewer repairs, no extra pressing charges, and you won't be buying unnecessary garments simply because you can't see the ones you have! Brooke Stoddard, a very organized design assistant at American *Harper's Bazaar*, has such a mania for visibility that she Polaroids each outfit and inserts the picture in a 'style diary'. She says, 'I can leaf through my book instead of through my closet when I'm contemplating what to wear.' Too much effort for most of us, but perhaps the idea may be a good one if you have the time, the interest, or a fashion-related career.

To organize your lean closet, here is the basic list of closetware you may need to purchase:

- **Dress, Skirt and Trousers Hangers**
- **Belt Holders**
- **Shoe Storage Units**
- **Handbag Storage Shelves or Boxes**
- **Scarf Hangers**
- **Sweater Boxes**

Hangers

I just about insist that any decent closet should be equipped with matching hangers. If you're wealthy and can afford fabulous scented, satin-upholstered ones, fine. But I just use the standard clear plastic ones with metal hooks that swivel. I prefer these to the more modern one-piece white (or colored) plastic variety. Those require you to be careful which direction your clothing goes on them. It is important when hanging clothing in your closet to have everything face in one direction. This isn't just my neurotic compulsiveness cropping up. Visibility is the name of the game. And hangers of different heights and styles will make it difficult for you to compare the lengths and the cuts of the jackets and dresses arrayed before you. Since, in most discount stores, you can buy a set of a dozen hangers for a lot less than five pounds, there is no excuse for leaving things on the wire disasters that dry cleaners distribute. Those hangers also tend to damage the clothes by snagging them on the sharp end of their twisted wire, potentially leaving rust stains, as well as deforming the shoulder line of delicate or knitted garments. Why pay for expensive pressing only to find the blouse hanging crookedly with creases mashed in?

Now that you no longer have your communion dress, girl guide uniform, your old maternity tops, and the blazer from your first job all squashed into the closet, it shouldn't take long to take your final selection of clothing and arrange it on identical hangers, face forward. This exercise will also help you to clarify just one more time what you have in abundance and what, if anything, you may be missing.

There are several different approaches to arranging the clothes in your closet. As I mentioned earlier, I believe it is easiest to hang an entire outfit - the trousers, blouse, and jacket or blazer that I usually wear together - on a single hanger. I go so far as to hang the scarf I wear with it on the hanger as well. For me, this arrangement works. I rarely substitute one piece for another, with one major exception – at the side of my closet I hang a couple of pairs of black trousers and a couple of skirts which I can substitute for any of the other bottoms in my collection.

My sister, on the other hand, is a bit more obsessive-compulsive. She hangs all of her jackets together, then has a section of blouses, followed by one of skirts and trousers. The advantage to this system is that you can see everything you own a bit more readily. The disadvantage is that you actually have to remember which items go with which.

Amy, who wears dresses or suits almost exclusively, uses a different but equally successful organizational method: she has all of her dresses and suits lined up by color, season, and silhouette. Her closet is really beautiful to look into.

And that's part of the point here. We are working together to try to make dressing both a pleasant and easy part of your day. Opening a closet door to a snake pit shambles, and rooting through it only to find that the skirt you need for the jacket you selected is at the cleaners, or that you simply cannot find the beige blouse you know has to be there, adds a nasty extra pressure to your already busy morning. When my closet is organized, I take pleasure in getting dressed, and when it isn't, I dress hurriedly, haphazardly and I end up unhappy with the results.

Belt Holders

*I*f you are going to wear belts, you have to find a way to display them for easy selection. There are all kinds of little gadgets in the marketplace: racks that can be attached to the back of a closet door, special hangers with belt holders attached, etc. Because I like to keep it simple (and because I don't have a lovely tiny waist) I only have two belts, a very expensive black leather one which I wear most often and a brown one. I keep these on a hook right at the front of the closet. But there are some other cloth belts that came with slacks or dresses. I simply keep these on the hanger with the garment they match. Whatever method you choose, the important principle is **everything must be visible or else you'll forget what you own.**

Shoe Storage Units

*A*s I mentioned earlier, just about every woman I know has a streak of Imelda Marcos in her. But who can afford to house three thousand pairs of shoes? I love the shoe salon – almost a whole floor – at Harrods. But I've gotten myself under control. I tried at first to store my pared-down pairs in the plastic hanging shoe bags sold by department stores and mail order catalogues.

They didn't work for me. I couldn't see the shoes and it was a pain in the neck to have to unzip the long plastic 'door' to get to them. Plus it took up a lot of valuable closet hanging space. After trying to keep them lined up on the closet floor (and invariably winding up with a dusty mess) I bit the bullet and got shoe racks. Each pair is now displayed neatly in its own compartment and I only have room for fourteen pairs of shoes (but that's not counting trainers). I don't know if that's a lot or a little, but they are very good shoes!

Find out what works for you. But don't keep shoes closed up in the cardboard boxes they came in. Our editor does this and says he likes to. But I believe you will forget what you have and nothing wastes more time when you're running late than digging through closed boxes like a maddened ferret, hunting for those green suede pumps you were sure you had in the front.

Handbag Storage Shelves or Boxes

*M*ost closets have what carpenters call 'hat shelves' (though I don't know of anyone besides Amy who puts hats there). These are the shelves immediately above the closet pole. I find them a perfect place to keep my handbags. This way, at a quick glance,

I can see which one I need to wear on a given day or evening. Don't keep them wrapped up in the bottom of a drawer. This is another way to forget what you have, buying more of something you already own.

Scarf Hangers

*D*id I mention that I love scarves?! Since I tend to wear neutral toned, fairly tailored clothing, I depend on scarves to give some movement and flow, some softness and femininity. And perhaps because of that I am more likely to be extravagant when it comes to buying a beautiful scarf than with any other purchase. (Since I wear them so often I feel the cost is justified.) But it has taken me a long time to find an efficient way to store them. I once read that Princess Grace stored her costly Hermès and Gucci scarves and shawls on trousers hangers, covering them first with acid-free tissue. Well, that's fine if you have the royal closet space, the time, the patience, or the staff, but I don't. My sister had special cabinets built that let her fold hers away in flat, shallow drawers but most of us don't have the money for that kind of effort, either. And I believe that folding scarves and hiding them in drawers makes it more difficult to remember what you have and how you wear them. My solution, as I mentioned earlier, is to drape them over the hanger holding the outfit I wear them with. Amy's solution is equally viable: she gently rolls them in clear plastic stackable drawers so they are visible and easily accessible. An artist friend of mine in Camden hangs her scarves and her necklaces on pegs all across her vast loft wall, where they make a wonderful display of color and pattern (although I would worry about dust and dirt settling on them).

Sweater Boxes

I love sweaters, but storing them has been the bane of my closets. If I fold them neatly and put them in dresser drawers I forget what I have and if I hang them beside my blouses, they stretch and lose their shape. The only answer that works for me is using the transparent plastic (yes, we hate plastic too) sweater boxes that I stack on the hat shelf of my closet. The benefits of these are that they protect sweaters from moths and dirt but keep them visible. Amy keeps her sweaters in cubbyholes (which she originally had constructed for filing her papers!). If anyone has a better solution do let us know.

And when you're tempted to buy more stuff, remember: **the most luxurious thing in your closet is space.**

CHAPTER THIRTEEN

Grooming and Maintenance

or Care and
Breeding

> *'She wears her clothes as if
> they were thrown on her
> with a pitchfork'*
> – JONATHAN SWIFT

*N*OW THAT
you have the beautiful
clothes and the beautifully
organized closet, you aren't done.
Just as a gorgeous painting can be
ruined through mishandling, so the portrait
of yourself that you have so masterfully created can be
spoiled if care isn't taken with these five basic points:

1. **Wardrobe Maintenance**

    2. **Haircare**

3. **Nail and Hand Grooming**

    4. **Skin Care and Makeup**

5. **Scents**

Because most of us have a life outside our closets and our bathrooms, *Simple Isn't Easy* here takes a deeply practical view: to keep maintenance high, but not too time-consuming, we almost always vote for the simple approach.

Wardrobe

*L*ike a purebred show dog with a mangy coat, a superb wardrobe will appear degraded if buttons are missing, linings are unraveling, collars are dingy and sweaters are piled. While superior quality clothes will wear better and last longer, they, like an expensive foreign car or a Cartier watch, require periodic tune-ups and proper maintenance. No less than its poor acrylic cousin, the most luxurious cashmere pullover can be spattered with tomato sauce, snagged on a prickly wicker chair, or frayed at the cuffs by regular wear. Diana Vreeland, whose band-box fresh, immaculate elegance continues to be an inspiration to everyone who knew her, said that the most heavenly scent on earth was the smell of saddle-soap on clean leather. She made a religion of grooming, loving all the implements and artisans associated with wardrobe maintenance, as well as the effects they produced. (Her maid actually polished the soles of her shoes, cleaned out the inside of her handbag, and laundered and pressed her dollar bills.) Vreeland once even went so far as to say that she could live anywhere as long as there was a good shoe repairman in town!

Well, few of us have Vreeland's means, or this level of fanaticism, nor do our jobs depend on our personal style as hers did. But we can still profit from her example. Cleanliness is not only next to godliness, it's also the most fundamental component of style. (Unless, of course, you're in a heavy metal band.) Nothing can undermine all the good style work you've done as completely as a grease stain on your lapel, or a run in your tights (and no nail polish touch-ups, please!).

The good news is that with fewer clothes, constant, vigilant stock-taking of your clothes' condition is not so onerous. With the contents of your closet streamlined, the hazards of mashed-in wrinkles, gaping seams, or silk dresses slipping off hangers to the closet floor are diminished. But care is still of the essence, and it's easiest to keep up with maintenance yourself, when possible. The basic tools to ensure upkeep must be kept on hand. They include:

A Good Quality Steam Iron

Keep a supply of the requisite accessories – a can of spray starch, an ironing board (tabletop models will do if space is limited), distilled water, etc. Pressing is definitely a minor art, and the price you pay for dry cleaning is twenty-five per cent cleaning and seventy-five per cent pressing labor, because ironing takes patience and skill. Although some of us find ironing a relaxing, satisfying activity, others are past masters of the slow burn and sizzle. If ironing seems nothing more than a burdensome chore, if fabrics are too delicate, or you're always in a hurry, consider purchasing the alternative:

A Professional Steamer

Yes, you know the kind we mean – the large
bulky models you see in boutiques, or,
alternatively, the hand-held, travel-size version.
Amy thought long and hard before buying one of
those upright steamers – it wasn't cheap and it
was space-consuming. But, as ironing is about as
appealing to her as grave-digging, she has never
regretted the purchase. And she's saved a fortune
in dry cleaning and pressing charges (while her
iron now languishes in the back of a kitchen
cabinet). Amy's sister, Erika, who has no room
for such a full-size industrial tool, instead wields
her travel steamer like a magic wand. And I
know a flight attendant with a great stall shower
– she hangs clothes from a hook she installed in
her bathroom ceiling and lets the rising steam do
the rest!

If you are really a slouch when it comes to
banishing wrinkles, there is a canned, spray-on
chemical product that does the trick. (Amy once
heard a woman in the hardware store asking if
the formula worked on faces too!) Of course,
none of the gizmos in this category will press a
razor-sharp crease into your trousers, so if you

hate ironing, maybe you should consider that
problem next time you want to buy a pair of
finely tailored trousers.

A Sweater Shaver (or a regular electric shaver)

Even if you like your man with a little stubble,
the attraction doesn't apply when it comes to
your sweaters. Some knits seem to sprout fuzz
faster than your armpits. Banish that two-day
growth with a sweater shaver, which operates
just like an electric razor. (We don't recommend
waxing or any form of cream depilatory!) But be
careful – shaving too often or too deep can nick
the delicate fibers just as a razor can nick your
skin. Except sweaters don't grow back!

A Lint Brush

A hairbrush-shaped tool, it dutifully collects all
that flotsam and jetsam that people like to pick
off your clothes when they're in an intimate
mood.

A Tape Roller

Slightly more primitive than the above, but
sometimes more effective. I keep one in the hall
closet, one in my desk drawer, one in my suitcase,
and one in the bathroom. But then, I have a cat and
a dog, along with a preference for dark colors that
attract everything but men and money. In a pinch
you can practice the sticky-fingers technique and
wrap masking tape or Sellotape around your pretty
hands – sticky side out – and go to work. (One
executive we know swears by self-stick mailing
labels.)

A Small Sewing Kit

Even if it's just for an emergency, like stitching up a
torn hem or securing a button that's about to take its
death plunge, you need the basics – straight pins,
needles, threads in a few colors. If sewing's not one
of the domestic arts you've mastered, at least keep
handy assorted safety pins for stopgap mending
until you find an obliging friend or professional
seamstress. And we don't have to tell you not to wait
too long – or that a stitch in time is a good idea.

A Button Box

Most clothes come with an extra button or two,
or even a bit of matching thread. Don't throw
these out or stuff them someplace where they'll
be forgotten or lost. Toss them into one large,
covered container. My sister taught me the value
of a button box, and I now have a pretty ceramic
one sitting on my bedroom bureau.

A Suede Brush, Suede Spray, and Spray Waterproofer

Don't let rain, mud, snow, or sleet ruin your
beautiful shoes and boots, even if they ruin your
day. Always have a pair of what we call 'rain
shoes' – patent leather or rubber shoes that can
take the weather – to spare your most precious
footwear from the elements. They don't have to
look like ducks' feet either. Search them out –
they are not only a life saver but a shoe-saver.

Because a well-made pair of shoes, well-tended,
can have a very long life, be sure to weather-

proof all your shoes before you wear them,
though it may alter the color slightly. The
healthier a patient is to start with, the better she
mends. As we reminded you earlier, the better
the quality of your shoes, the more responsive
they are to good care.

A Tin or Tube of Neutral Leather Cream

You don't need a big shoe polish box and a host
of different colors. Just a little soft rag, one tin of
neutral polish and a lot of elbow grease – for
leather or suede handbags and belts as well as
shoes.

Spot Remover

A must for on-the-spot stain removal. Every
couture workroom has stashes of them. As
designer Gene Meyer says, 'Full dry-cleaning can
remove spots, but also take the life out of
clothes.'

Professionals You Can Trust

Perhaps most important of all are the old reliables: a good, attentive dry cleaner, a seamstress or tailor, and a good cobbler. Though more expensive than the previous solutions, they are often worth it, especially if you have little faith in your own abilities. Expert help is almost always available for a price. Think of these professionals as your clothes doctors. And, as with physicians, it's best to bring your ailing shoes and garments in to the experts at the earliest sign of distress. Prevention is the best medicine.

Hair

*T*here are so many jokes about bad hair days, epidemiologists should classify them as a plague. The truth is, when your hair looks awful, so do you. But here's the good news: There is no bad hair, only bad haircuts. And there are only two simple (but not easy) rules: **get a great cut** and **keep it clean.**

If you are trying to model your hairdo after a photo in a magazine or the coiffure of a favorite TV star, be warned. First of all, that look you admire has been created for a short-lived camera session by a battalion of specialists who are fooling with lights, cameras, curlers and clips. Unless you have space in your bathroom to bunk a team of pros, forget it! And that Big Hair that you see on soap stars and female television newscasters is larger than life for a purpose: the TV camera likes exaggeration. What looks right on the small screen is disproportionate in real life. We guarantee that your favorite star's hair looks very different in her private life. So get a good, realistic cut that follows your hair's natural inclination.

The Cut

The lack of a good haircut can not only
undermine your self-confidence, it can also ruin
your credibility. But how to get a good hair cut?
We all know the horror stories: he promised you
the moon but gave you terminal frizzies. It takes
some time and experimentation to find a
competent, *sympatico*, attentive hairdresser, but
it can be done. Try to find someone who studies
your face, your personality and your life, as well
as your hair type, and cuts accordingly. And
beware of the gal or guy who gives the same cut
to everyone; cookie-cutter hair trends that flatter
some clients, but do nothing for others. Also
avoid those pushy dictators who manipulate you
and make you feel insecure (well, avoid anyone
who does that!). Amy's hairstylist told her that,
sadly, many women subjugate themselves to bad
hairdressers because there doesn't seem to be
anyone else in their life who ever talks to them
or touches them so intimately. I remember one
very handsome haircutter I went to who finished
by putting his hands on my shoulders, rubbing
seductively and telling me I looked beautiful. (I
didn't, and I didn't go back.)

Both Amy and I urge you to judge your hairdresser's work by how it looks right after a cut and simple dry, not after he or she twiddles and sprays and blows and backcombs it. Stylish hair is all about a cut appropriate to your hair texture. If stylists have to doctor your locks with curling irons, gels, mousse, and other goopy products, they are just covering up their shortcomings. You won't be able to reproduce that look at home. Forget most potions and lotions. They're labor-intensive, expensive, and rarely live up to their promises. Remember the point of *Simple Isn't Easy*: take the time to get it simple and right, then stick to it. You should be able to style your hair at home with just a brush, comb, blow dryer, and – at most – a little dab of product and a few squirts of spray. (If you find yourself staring hopelessly into the mirror each morning, yearning for a wig, you are definitely on the wrong track.) Also, remember that hair salons make a lot of profit by selling these highly marked-up products which so often end up collected and unused. If your hairdresser keeps pushing you to buy, find another.

Coloring and Perms

Generally, the rule here is respect your hair's natural color and texture, and it will behave kindly to you in return! With few exceptions, drastic departures from what nature endowed you with will never produce the results you desire. And they are never simple or easy to accomplish. There are beautiful, looks-enhancing styles for every hair type. In general, it's best not to be in a battle against your kinks, your curls, or your ramrod straight hair. It's a losing fight. Fried, frizzled hair – overbleached and overpermed – rarely looks stylish. Most of us are simply too prone to the grass is greener (or curlier, or blonder, or redder) syndrome. Have you ever noticed that the curly-headed want straight hair, the straight-haired want curls, the thick-tressed want fine hair, and the fine-haired want volume? (OK, we admit that blondes never want to be brunettes, but they have to put up with 'dumb-blonde' jokes.) Carried to its logical conclusion, we have to deduce that all hair types are desirable to someone. Make peace with yours. Remember, self-acceptance is the basic condition for style.

As far as covering the grey goes, we know women who do and women who don't. You can look great either way. But many women feel that grey hair is aging, and it certainly will change the way your makeup and clothes look. If you feel you must color the grey, then be sure to keep up with the roots; nothing looks worse than partly-colored hair.

Eyebrows

And while we're on hair, don't forget to groom your eyebrows too, by plucking, combing or coloring as your look dictates. Eyebrows give the face a great deal of its expression and definition. Fabulous faces have distinctive brows: think of Elizabeth Taylor, Brooke Shields, Audrey Hepburn, Linda Evangelista.

Nails

*S*hort and soft is just right for a pair of ankle
socks, but it's hardly what we strive for in our
nails. My nails are baby soft and tear like paper. Amy's
split, peel, and break before they reach the end of her
fingertips, and since early adolescence she has tried
every remedy, from gelatin drinks to glues, wraps, tips,
and powders. (The drink didn't hurt, but all the other
messy fixes were time-consuming, expensive, and finally
unhealthy.)

Amy found a manicurist who, like a skilled gardener,
got rid of all the artifice, and helped her to cultivate
healthier nails. She forced her to wear them short, and
merely buffed, with no polish. After all those years of
wearing scarlet on her fingertips, Amy was surprised to
behold her bare hands. But now she loves them. The
look is clean, simple, and chic, and she can rush out of
the salon without that agonizingly long drying session.

I let my nails grow a bit, but use a nail strengthener, not
just a polish. I use a neutral color so I don't have to
worry about my fingertips clashing with my coat, or my
polish chipping. What a relief!

Good grooming means your nails must be clean, your cuticles and hangnails well-tended. If your nails are naturally strong, and take polish and longer lengths well, fine and wonderful. Otherwise, retract those Dragon Lady claws. (Incidentally, if you look at magazine photos of models, you will seldom see very long nails.) But if varnished talons are part of your trademark style, that's fine. Just don't wind up looking like Dame Edna Everage! And remember – always keep them neat. Chipped polish is to fingers what runs are to stockings. It's a sure way to mar your carefully cultivated look.

Pedicures may not be quite as visible or important as manicures, but consider: feet are not usually the fine point of our anatomy yet we depend on them for locomotion, and all too often stuff them in shoes that are too tight, too high, and too pointy. Then we wonder why our dogs bark. Keep them free of calluses, hangnails, etc, and cut, file, buff or polish those ten little piggies. (By the way, the red Amy used to wear on her fingers now goes on her toes!) If you are thinking, 'Well, it's just too much trouble, after all, nobody sees my toes except me,' take this advice from Gloria Vanderbilt. When, as a young girl, she asked an older woman why she wore such lovely, expensive underwear when no one saw it, her friend said, 'But I do!'. It's a good mantra to apply universally – to the linings of your jackets, the inside of your handbag, and to all that is hidden from everyone but you. You are your most important audience.

Skin

F. Scott Fitzgerald wrote, 'Let me tell you about the very rich. They are different from you and me.' He was right, but only in one important respect: They have better skin.

Nothing compares with the look of clean, clear, well-moisturized, glowing skin. This is one of the few areas where American women seem to outstrip their UK sisters. As Chrissy Bourne of Surrey put it, 'In the US I always notice that stylish women seem to have better groomed bodies – better tone, better skin. We're just catching up here with nails, hair color, and the like.' Almost every celebrity we have seen in person has that one trait in common – flawless skin. The camera loves it. Are they born with it or do they acquire it through good habits? Do constant saunas, steam baths, facials, and exercise create that glow? We don't know for sure, but if you weren't lucky enough to be blessed with the genes you deserve, then at least practice the hygiene that will bring the best out of yours.

No artist would paint a beautiful picture over a mottled, grease-stained canvas, so why apply makeup over ill-kempt skin? The glow of skin, like the light of a diamond, shines from beneath the surface. Skin cleanliness is not only about keeping the outermost layer dirt-free with good soaps and lotions. It is about deeper cleaning – getting out all the oil, dirt and dead cells embedded in your pores. This is tricky to do on your own, but steaming and masks will help. If it's at all possible to spend the money – you have, after all, saved a bundle on clothing, hair and nail products already! – get regular professional facials.

A good facial isn't about patting and rubbing your face – it's about opening the pores, cleaning out whiteheads and blackheads and then closing pores and toning the skin. It's not always a pleasant process, having someone peer at the side of your nose through a magnifying glass as they press out old dirt, but it is worth it. If the facialist is good, it shouldn't hurt much nor should your face be red as a strawberry when you walk out. And, like your hairdresser, she shouldn't be too pushy with products either. (A very useful tip: Many dermatologists employ a facialist whose services are covered by insurance.)

Meanwhile, don't be fooled and shamed by department store saleswomen who wipe your face with a product and show you the results – a grey cotton ball. No, you are not filthy. We all are constantly shedding the top layer of skin and it looks grey on the cotton. Big deal! That kind of wiping does not do deep cleansing.

Because the point here is to keep it simple, once your skin is clean, it doesn't need much else. Most dermatologists agree that a single moisturizer can do the work of an eye cream, a day cream, and a night cream, (though Amy insists on all three).

If you have chronic problems with acne or rashes, or have bad pock marks that bother you, we urge you to consult a first-rate dermatologist, or, if necessary, a topflight plastic surgeon to get whatever help you can. (One tip: avoid plastic surgeons who advertise. The best doctors get their patients from referrals by other satisfied clients or other doctors.) With all physicians, a hospital or academic affiliation is one important sign of competence. A good dermatologist will tell you that ninety per cent of the promises on commercial skin products are either outright lies or exaggerations. My dermatologist got me over an embarrassing (and late-to-bloom) case of acne that struck me at thirty. No cosmetics helped. What I needed was doctor-prescribed medicines. Now, no problems.

Makeup

*N*ow that your skin is looking lovelier, what to put on it? Makeup, like clothing, is an indicator of personality and another means of self-expression. To start, you need to know how you want to look. Once again, this is where some contemplation is necessary. Who are you? What do you really look like and how do you want to appear? As we recommended for your wardrobe, the goal here is to know yourself, simplify your approach, and find a makeup routine and stick with it.

Long ago Amy gave up her paintbrushes to write. But every morning she still picks up her makeup brushes and goes to work, creating a self-portrait. The art of applying makeup begins with the tools. Cosmetics are only as good as the implements used to apply them.

Start out with a good set of brushes – and then go through your mounds of makeup like a *Simple Isn't Easy* pro. That blue liner that you bought five tubes of five years ago when you were convinced it was the secret to beautiful eyes – into the trash. The twelve colors of blusher? Nobody needs more than two. The eyelash curler that you mean to use every morning, but you run out of time? In the garbage. The sparkly green shadow that you used in the sixth form and are saving for the next costume party – wastebasket fodder. Those makeup kits with the seven hundred colors, stubby little tools, and stunted mascara that dried up the week you bought it – none of these hold the key to a pared-down routine. Once you've sorted through your cosmetic chest, examine what's left – the stuff you actually use. (We hope more than a single cottonwool bud!) Look once more through the dregs and see what else you can toss. Whatever is left could be the basis of your daily makeup ritual.

And forget the old fashioned idea of 'a different look for evening'. Your day makeup, with a slight increase in intensity, will suffice. Think of all the time and money and shelf-space you save.

SOME BASIC MAKEUP TIPS:

Get a makeup sponge

One tip that almost anyone can benefit from is
to use a sponge to apply foundation. Fingers just
don't do the job. Amy uses 'wonder wedges', by
the dozen. I prefer tiny natural sea sponges. And
throw them out often. Dirty sponges are
breeding grounds for skin problems.

When you find a product or a look that works, stick with it

As with clothing, if one day your face is pale
and lips are carmine, while the next you go for a
bottle-based California tan, you don't have a
look. We see lots of faces we admire, from the
most natural 'non-made-up' makeup to stylized
extremes. But a new face each day can be
unsettling.

Avoid 'free' make-overs

They are usually nothing more than product-pushing. (They always paint me up like a clown, anyway.) The old expression that when you pay nothing, you get what you pay for applies here. If you really are unsatisfied with your current makeup regimen, find a skilled cosmetologist, pay for the session, and learn to apply it.

Ignore those ubiquitous gift-with-purchase promotions

Unless the product given away is one you actually already use and like – notice that they rarely are – forget about 'gifts' and giveaways. Invariably, you wind up buying more stuff than you need to get a useless gift. And it all clutters up your makeup shelf, which should be as streamlined and organized as your closet.

Buy multiples of a favorite product

Since colors are often discontinued, buy what
you like in quantity. Store the extra makeup in
the refrigerator to ensure freshness and
longevity.

Don't swap makeup

Eye infections, herpes, acne and rashes are all
contagious. There's no reason for using anyone
else's mascara or lipstick, ever.

Lip pencils or lip liners

Used under lipstick, these prolong the staying
power of your lip color.

As a general rule, makeup should be used to enhance or exaggerate facial features that you want to draw attention to, rather than to hide what you don't like or create what you don't have. 'The best way to look good is to enhance what one already has, simply and easily,' says makeup-artist-to-the-stars Kevyn Aucoin. Unless you're going kabuki, don't paint on a second face. Dark slashes will not fool anyone into believing you have cheekbones or deep-set eyelids where there are none. Thin lips will just look a mess if you draw an outline far outside your natural lip line to pretend they are fuller. This makeup-as-camouflage technique sometimes works for photos, but not real life. As Evy, a makeup artist with MAC cosmetics, says, 'You want people to look at your eyes, not your eye makeup.'

Amy likes to slightly exaggerate her natural pallor with foundation, powder, and dark-red lipstick, and accentuate her almond-shaped eyes with dark, slanting liner on the upper lid only. I emphasize my large round eyes with contouring shadows, and keep my lips, which already have a lot of natural pigment, relatively pale. Our approaches are very different but they have one thing in common: we both have our makeup routine down pat. If we can't quite get made up with our eyes shut, we at least can get through that A.M. paint-and-powder session with a minimum of thought – and hardly any time. As Diana Vreeland, who could apply her Chinese-red lipstick perfectly without even a glance in the mirror, said, 'Do you think that after all these years I don't know where these old lips are?'

The style of your makeup should take its cues from the style of your clothes (both based, of course, on the identity you have found for yourself, thanks to *Simple Isn't Easy*). Amy likes a certain amount of exotic artifice, in keeping with her urbane, very stylized, high-fashion wardrobe. Her makeup and clothing are almost like a fashion drawing. My cosmetic palette, like that of my wardrobe, is all about low-key neutrals. Is your style sporty, girlish, businesslike, tailored, flamboyant? Figure it out, and then be sure your makeup complements your persona.

We don't have to mention that outdoorsy clothes don't go with eyes laden with starry lashes and lips sparkling with magenta frost. A scrubbed, bare face won't do with satin flounces and bows. And don't match your makeup colors to your wardrobe. No turquoise eyeliner to match your belt. Your makeup colors should take their cue from your hair and skin coloring, not your poison-green pullover. The shades you choose should be universal enough to go with everything you wear. And what's this thing about lipstick? Do they multiply in the medicine cabinet? Every woman I know has twenty, though they don't wear most of them. At the most have two or three lipstick shades – one to contrast with your complexion, another to blend with it.

If you resist all advice about makeup, then do yourself a favor and at least heed these two most basic suggestions:

1. Blend, blend, blend – no lines of demarcation for blusher, powder, foundation, shadows – for the most professional finish

Amy swears by translucent face powder beneath and on top of her makeup to achieve this polished effect. Of course, all rules are made to be broken and I did see a young girl with Day-Glo orange lips and thin, orange lines painted along her upper lashes. She looked fabulous, but it's not for everyone. And she was under seventeen.

2. Take ten to fifteen minutes *maximum* putting on your makeup – otherwise something is wrong

If your routine isn't quick, it's too complicated. Or you're simply wearing too much makeup. Unless, of course, you like that Barbara Cartland look, and then you're on your own.

Scents

A woman's scent should be both wonderful and
mysterious. And, like any good mystery, it
shouldn't be obvious from ten feet away. A perfume
should neither announce your arrival, nor leave behind
a trail like a diesel's exhaust. It should be semi-private,
inhaled only by those whose privilege it is to come close
to you. A Frenchman we know fondly recalls how on the
first day of school his *maman* tucked her perfume-
scented handkerchief into his pocket so that he wouldn't
feel too lonely for her. This touching tale could never
apply to a woman with multiple perfume personalities.

Scents are powerful and often unconscious manipu-
lators. Whenever I smell library paste I think of my
kindergarten classroom and Mrs Ackerman, my teacher.
And they can be invisible turn-offs as well. Once, as a
teenager, I had a huge crush on a poetic blond boy who
avoided me. Years later, after college, we met again and
he confessed he hated the smell of my face – an
inoffensive skin cleanser that, unfortunately for me,
reminded him of his dad's aftershave!

A scent is linked with your identity, so we suggest that you find one and remain faithful. It's more sophisticated and much simpler. Pay no attention to those perfume purveyors who tell you to have a morning scent, an evening scent and a scent for each season. They are already selling the fashion industry's most highly marked-up product.

But once again, don't buy cheap brands, or nasty knock-offs of famous brands. Their scent often changes over time as it reacts with your skin. As my friend Connie insists, 'Honest body odor smells a hell of a lot better than stink water.' (And don't you think it's odd that a certain skin lotion is used as a no-fail bug repellent? What, we ask, does it attract?) Finally, don't make the mistake of letting other scented products fight against your signature scent. You weaken and confuse your olfactory image when you layer on scented hair spray, deodorant, skin cream, and bath gel. Buy coordinated products, or 'scent-free' ones.

Remember, with perfume, simple is not only easier, it is the only way to go.

CHAPTER FOURTEEN

Changing Your Style

or What? After All This Work?

> *'Attachment is the great
> fabricator of illusions;
> reality can be attained only
> by someone who is
> detached'*
>
> – SIMONE WEIL

HERE COMES a time in many women's lives when a change in style is in order. Such a moment may occur after a divorce, a career change, a significant birthday, relocation, major hair recoloring, motherhood or a new marriage. You feel like moulting your old, tired skin and showing off a fresh new one.

So even though you have now found yourself in your closet and discovered your best personal style, there's still a chance you may one day outgrow it. This is not to say that any time the circumstances of your life alter you must reinvent yourself. We think of this future event – if it happens – not as a schizophrenic-like switching of identities but as a healthy, usually subtle evolution from one phase of your life to another.

And – even if your life doesn't take on a new dramatic turn – there are shifts in taste and fashion that inevitably occur over time. No, we hasten to remind you, we are not advocating jumping on top of every new trend. We simply mean updating, or editing a bit. So, if you have found a tried-and-true, enduring look for yourself, you probably will find that in order not to look frozen in time, like a prehistoric ant preserved in amber, you will need to make slight, periodic adjustments to update your style. We've all seen many a little lady trundling up the avenue, a victim of what Amy calls 'image arrest'. Amy remembers in particular seeing an ash blonde with a beehive hairdo, false eyelashes, frosted pink lipstick, in a short, fitted, leopard coat, her look freeze-framed circa 1962. But the year was 1982! And though she was a charmingly eccentric sight, she also inspired pity. These 'image arrest' women seem to

be communicating through their clothes, hair and
makeup that they were last happy two, three or four
decades ago.

Let me reiterate: we do not advise following every trend
to try to keep up with fashion. You'll only end up
looking like a fad-follower, not a woman of style.
Remember Yves St Laurent's words, 'Fashion changes
but style is eternal'. If you look at photographs of stylish
women over the decades you will notice only in retro-
spect how they update their style. They achieved a goal
of personal style despite the paradox presented by
fashion. They kept changing yet remaining the same. Of
course, many had the luxury of being able to afford to
wear whatever they wanted, and yet each had picked a
fairly consistent look. As the designer Valentino, who
dressed Jackie Onassis for many years, notes, 'Almost by
magic, Jackie Onassis kept in fashion without
significantly altering her look. Maybe the pant lengths
varied a little bit, the hair got longer or shorter, the skirt
length changed a few inches. But the look was consistent,
constant and fabulous in an outdoorsy American way.'

Updating gradually is the ideal way to keep your style,
without either scrabbling after trends or falling into the
sad trap of 'image arrest'. The paradox is that a classic

ust change somewhat to remain endlessly attractive to the contemporary eye. It's a company secret that the classic cubic Chanel No. 5 perfume bottle is, every now and then, slightly modified to ensure that its 'timeless design' never dates. In the Art Deco period, the flask had sharp, hard edges, but by the Fifties, when industrial design tastes changed, the bottle had become more rounded so it didn't seem out of place among the fat curves of automobiles and kidney-shaped coffee tables. Yet, despite its small variations, the bottle has never lost its identity, and nobody even noticed it change. This principle, if we could apply it to ourselves, would be the perfect approach. As writer Annette Tapert, author of *The Power of Style*, says, 'You don't invent yourself once and for all. Style is an ongoing creative process.'

Unfortunately, none of us has a team of industrial designers to tweak our style when necessary. How did they know when to update the Chanel bottle? How do you know when your look has grown stale? Here's a handy questionnaire that may help.

If you mark one 'yes', consider a change. If you've checked 'yes' two or more times, definitely give it a shot. Consult this list again a year from now, or every so often.

? Have you made a major physical change lately (lost a lot of weight, changed hair style or color etc.)?

? Are you readjusting after moving to another climate?

? Do you need to create a wardrobe for pregnancy or motherhood?

? Do you need to change your wardrobe to suit a new job?

? Does the need for change strike you with the force of a revelation?

? Is there is a consensual tide that you can no longer stem?

Putting Together a New Wardrobe
after Physical Change

*N*eedless to say, if you lose a lot of weight, gain it, or change your looks in any other major way, (cosmetic surgery, major hair style renovation, etc.) your wardrobe will (or should) be affected. When an older friend of ours simply decided to stop dyeing her hair and let it grow in a fabulous silver, she found that very few of her clothes looked the same. She'd gone from a dramatic brunette to an equally dramatic but very pale look. Her clothes had to change. If you go blonde, if you tan, even if you make a dramatic change in your makeup, hairstyle, or contact lens color, you may have to rethink at least some of your wardrobe and that may mean shopping. But not before you go back to chapter three and start over.

Readjusting after Moving to Another Climate

After years in New York and London, I moved down to Florida and found that I didn't have the right clothes. It wasn't just that I needed to trade my wool trousers for linen ones. I discovered that the sunlight, the lifestyle and the expectations were different in Florida. People dressed more casually than I did in the daytime, but got more dressy than I was used to at night. Weird. It took me a while to figure out what would work, especially given the complication that I always needed a sweater or jacket to cope with the air conditioning. If you relocate, you may find that you need to rethink your wardrobe completely. But don't rush into it. Make do with one or two new outfits from your preexisting spring and summer wardrobes until you figure out what will work. By day I still dress more formally than a lot of Floridians, and I'm still not in sequins at night, but my wardrobe *is* different. And I'm comfortable with it.

Creating a Wardrobe for Your Pregnancy Or Motherhood

*A*my says pregnancy is difficult enough without adding the burden of not knowing what to wear! Those castoffs that friends lend you and those potato sacks that mothers-in-law buy are guaranteed to be more nauseating than morning sickness. Nancy Robinson, who worked on this manuscript, told us, 'I was given a maternity dress by my sister and it was enormous! I already felt pretty immense, but when I put that dress on, I felt like I needed a 'Wide Load' sign across my behind.'

Lots of women try to get through their pregnancies without shopping at all – since there are already so many extra expenses. But they often end up depressed and depressing-looking – not to mention uncomfortable – in stretched-out sweaters and floppy old shirts. Instead, using our Simple Isn't Easy philosophy, remember that one or two good-looking dresses are better than a pile of ugly borrowed or cheaply-bought goods.

On the other hand, pregnancy can be a time to incubate a permanent new style. My friend Miriam discarded her stagnating vampy look – high heels, heavy liner, red lips – during her first pregnancy and continued her new look once she became a full-time mother. A practical soul, she never looked back. 'I feel much more myself now in flats, and no eye makeup – it just started to feel too heavy on me,' she says. With her very dark, well-defined features, and her ballerina's grace, she will never look dowdy in this new, simplified, stylish – but more motherly – guise.

Other changes may take place. To her horror, Amy's feet grew a size after pregnancy, and she has been gradually rebuilding her shoe wardrobe ever since. (At last! A legitimate excuse to buy shoes!) Finally, realize that you may already have suitable maternity wear in your closet. Amy found that most of her clothing with no defined waist (i.e. loose dresses, big jackets) saw her through her entire pregnancy. The only real maternity wear she bought were skirts. And don't listen to comments about how the hemline on a nonmaternity dress will rise higher in the front than the back. Who cares? It looks cute. You are pregnant, after all.

Changing Your Wardrobe to Suit a New Job

*D*iana Vreeland's life, says a former colleague, could be neatly divided into 'the turban phase, the snood phase, and the Alexandre haircut period'. She wore the turban when she was a young married lady of leisure. She adopted the snood when she began working as fashion editor for *Harper's Bazaar*. When she took over as editor-in-chief of *Vogue*, she lost the headgear and wore a sleek hairdo, invented by the great French hairdresser Alexandre. She kept that hairdo – which *Vogue's* creative director Andre Leon Talley calls, 'the black Kabuki flip' – for the rest of her days. The lesson to benefit from here is: be never quite in style, and never quite out of style. And always have a style that makes sense for your job.

The Need for Change Strikes You with the Force of a Revelation. ▼

A fashion editor friend of Amy's says that sometimes she puts on an outfit that looked exactly right a season or two ago, and suddenly, it seems all wrong – shoulders too big, length too long, silhouette too baggy. 'It's like discovering a stranger where there once was a friend,' she says. Maybe you've experienced that odd awakening. This probably means that, without your even quite knowing it, your eye has readjusted to changes in fashion or your self-image, while your wardrobe hasn't yet caught up. Amy's fashion editor friend compares that sudden revelation with the experience we've all had of, in a flash, realizing it's time for a haircut. 'The day before your hair seemed just fine,' she says. 'And overnight, everything seems to be falling in the wrong place. There's a gap between what exists in your mind's eye, and what you see in the mirror.'

My friend Cynthia has a clever approach to updates, 'I have a uniform, but each new season I try one new thing. Last year it was a pair of spikey, high-heeled shoes. It's not a big investment, but it gives you a chance to update and experiment with your basic look. So, can we, after all this, be telling you to throw stuff out the minute it 'goes out of style'? Of course not! Take that no-longer-loveable outfit and try retiring it for a while. I know an advertising account executive who buys only high-style designer suits but does tire of them. Still, she never throws them away. 'I put them in the hall closet for a vacation,' she says. 'Then, sometimes after a year or two, sometimes longer, they look fresh again.' And if they don't – off to the thrift shop.

There Is a Consensual Tide that You Can No Longer Stem

*A*my had a friend, Andrea, who was a borderline image arrest case. Andrea looked quite young, but one makeup habit of hers fixed her age as surely as a number around her neck. She wore dark lip liner which outlined a much paler shade of lipstick. Amy searched her soul every time she saw Andrea, thinking

of a delicate way to advise her to match lip liner to
lipstick shade, but the words failed her. She even talked
to me about it, but I advised her to keep her mouth shut!
(A girlfriend once told me my hair color looked 'cheap'
and I've never forgiven her!) Then, to Amy's surprise and
relief, one day Andrea showed up with a single, uniform
color upon her lips. 'I've had so many people tell me to
drop the dark lip liner,' Andrea explained to Amy without
her even having to ask. 'I just never thought I could get
used to seeing myself any other way. But I'm so glad I
listened – I now see how much better I look.'

If you hear over and over the same chorus of advice
from disparate, well-intentioned friends (or well-
meaning strangers), you might want to consider trying
out that recommendation, to cut or color your hair,
shorten your skirt, add eyebrow pencil – whatever. Amy
has had the courage, by the way, to point out gently to a
few extremely close friends, including her sister, that it
might in fact be time to pluck their eyebrows, or grow
them out, or reevaluate the use of a curling iron. She
changed her entire makeup routine herself after a pre-
party cosmetic session with a trustworthy friend, and
every now and then she asks that same friend if another
change is due.

CHAPTER FIFTEEN

In Closing

*A*ND THAT,
dear Reader, is that. You
have all the information
and motivation you could
possibly need to create and
keep an effective and stylish
wardrobe going. I'm sure you agree
that while our solutions, suggestions and
recommendations have been simple, they have
not been easy. But at this point you should be launched
on a new, more comfortable and more organized way of
dressing. And hey, isn't that you in the mirror looking
stylish, with a style that's all your own!

Letter to Readers

Did *Simple Isn't Easy* help you? We're interested in knowing how you applied our ideas to your own life.

Do you have any tricks of your own that women might benefit from? We would like to incorporate some reader responses into a new edition of *Simple Isn't Easy*. Please send your comments, suggestions and questions to us, care of our publisher:

> HarperCollins Publishers,
> 77-85 Fulham Palace Road,
> Hammersmith,
> London
> W6 8JB.

Sincerely and stylishly,

Olivia Goldsmith

Amy Fine Collins

P.S. Send us before and after pictures, of yourself and your closet!